OCR

A LEVEL
MUSIC

Revision
Guide

First published 2017 in Great Britain by
Rhinegold Education
14-15 Berners Street
London W1T 3LJ, UK
www.rhinegoldeducation.co.uk

© 2017 Rhinegold Education
a division of Music Sales Limited

> You should always check the current
> requirements of your examination, since
> these may change.

Editor: Sarah Lambie
Cover and book design: Fresh Lemon Australia

OCR A Level Music Revision Guide
Order no. RHG283
ISBN 978-1-78558-165-6

Exclusive Distributors:
Music Sales Ltd
Distribution Centre, Newmarket Road
Bury St Edmunds, Suffolk IP33 3YB, UK

Printed in the EU

OCR

A LEVEL MUSIC

Revision Guide

HUW ELLIS-WILLIAMS

RHINEGOLD
EDUCATION

Contents

The author

Huw Ellis-Williams

was brought up in Bangor and read Music at the University of Oxford. He was Head of Music and Head of Sixth Form at a comprehensive school in north Wales. He has examined for OCR and was a part of the team that wrote the OCR specifications for AS and A level Music. A pianist, organist and occasional composer, Huw enjoys being involved with the local community as a conductor and accompanist.

Introduction

About the A Level

The A Level in Music is made up of three activities:

- **Performing**
- **Composing**
- **Listening and appraising**

The OCR specification (H543) consists of five components, from which you choose three. You must take one route in performing and composing, either A or B:

Either

| Component 01 Performing A | **25%** |
| and Component 03 Composing A | **35%** |

Or

| Component 02 Performing B | **35%** |
| and Component 04 Composing B | **25%** |

You must also sit a written examination (05 Listening and appraising). This is worth **40%** of the total marks.

Using this book

This revision guide focuses mainly on the three sections (A, B and C) of the written exam.

It contains:

- Material to help you with the unprepared listening in Section A
- Advice for revising the prescribed works in Section B
- Guidance for revising and writing essays in Section C.

It also includes some advice on preparing for your performing recital and on completing your compositions.

The A Level course is intended for study over a period of two years. This gives you time to develop your skills as a musician. Spend as much time as you can extending your abilities as a performer and composer. Listen to music of all kinds and be open to new ideas.

In the end, however, the A Level qualification is assessed on the work you do in the exam.

The examiners can only mark what they see and hear:

- The video recording of your performing recital
- The audio recording of your compositions and the scores/written material you submit as your coursework
- The answers that you write in the 2½ hours of the exam.

The aim of this book is to help you with the requirements of the exam. The specification and the OCR website include details of what you need to know and the skills that you should demonstrate. There are also sample questions and mark schemes which show you what the examiners want to know and how they award the marks.

The full specification for your A Level, along with sample papers and mark schemes, can be found on OCR's website, here: www.ocr.org.uk/qualifications/as-a-level-gce-music-h143-h543-from-2016/

Areas of Study

The areas of study for the A Level qualification are as follows:

Area of Study 1	Instrumental Music of Haydn, Mozart and Beethoven
Area of Study 2	Popular Song: Blues, Jazz, Swing and Big Band
Area of Study 3	Developments in Instrumental Jazz 1910 to the present day
Area of Study 4	Religious Music of the Baroque Period
Area of Study 5	Programme Music 1820–1910
Area of Study 6	Innovations in Music 1900 to the present day

Preparation for A Level Music: Top ten tips

1. Engage in wider listening: explore

2. Be confident about challenges

3. Use your time in the first year to develop as a musician

4. Work with other musicians, perform for an audience, try out your compositions with live musicians

5. Make connections between the three activities: performing, composing and the written exam – OCR wants you to integrate

6. Practise musical skills in performing and composing

7. Develop a good writing style

8. Develop an opinion – justify your ideas, debate with others

9. Plan the final year of the course: meeting deadlines for composing, preparing for the recital, revising for the exam

10. Revise methodically for each of your chosen Areas of Study.

Good luck!

Performing

About the component

You should discuss with your teacher at school or college whether to choose Performing A (35%) or Performing B (25%). Your choice will depend on your strengths and interests. Do you prefer performing or composing? Which are you more confident about?

- Performing A (25%) consists of a recital of 6–9 minutes in length. If you choose it, you must also choose Composing A (35%).
- Performing B (35%) consists of a recital of 10–15 minutes. If you choose it, you must also choose Composing B (25%).

Component	% of marks	Recital		Total length
Performing A	25%	- Free choice - At least two *contrasting* pieces - 75 marks		6–9 minutes
Performing B	35%	**Section 1** - Free choice - At least two *contrasting* pieces - 75 marks	**Section 2** - Focused study - At least one piece - 30 marks	10–15 minutes

Top ten tips for performing

1. Select your pieces carefully

Look for contrasting pieces (for example fast and slow, loud and soft, or differing styles or genres of music). Since the exam board encourages integration of your learning across the syllabus, you may choose a recital programme related to one of your chosen Areas of Study for the written paper. This might be useful to help you to demonstrate your understanding of style and context, and to inform your choice of pieces.

2. Your recital should demonstrate a variety of techniques

These might include legato and staccato, high and low registers, and so on.

3. You need some challenge in your recital, but avoid pieces that are too difficult

Choose music that you can play accurately without having to slow down or hesitate in the more difficult passages. Don't automatically choose your Grade 8 exam pieces if they're too difficult for you. However you *should* choose pieces which require the equivalent level of technical skill to the repertoire from syllabuses of the performing examining bodies at Grade 6. You might choose pieces of this standard from the ABRSM, TCL, LCM, Rockschool, Trinity Rock and Pop, and Yamaha syllabuses, and so on. If the music performed is not Grade 6 level or above, then you won't be able to reach the top two mark bands for 'technical control'.

4. Rehearse thoroughly with other musicians, if there are any

This might include the accompanist, or the others in an ensemble. Give them their music well in advance. They will want to practise, just like you!

5. Make sure the camera recording your recital has a good view of you

The examiner will want to see you perform: don't hide your hands behind the lid of the piano, for example.

6. Check the balance

If you are in a group, your part needs to be heard clearly as it is you who is being examined.

7. Check the tuning of instruments very carefully

Don't let poor intonation affect the performance.

8. Plan how to deal with your nerves

This is especially important if you usually get anxious about performing. There are strategies to cope with performance anxiety. Do some research on these. Talk to your teacher about how you can make the recital go as smoothly as possible.

9. Take part in other recitals to build up your performing experience

Get used to the routine of a performance: rehearsal, last minute preparation, warming-up and tuning, performing for an audience and recording your own performances, introducing your programme, acknowledging the audience's applause.

10. Record your performances

You will find that this is a valuable way of improving your work. You can listen to your performance critically and think of ways you can improve, not only in the accuracy but also the communication of the music. You might think that you are adding sufficient dynamics and suitable phrasing but until you listen to yourself you might be unaware that more is needed.

What the examiners are looking for

Performing A / Performing B: Section 1

You are expected to show:

- Knowledge and fluency (25 marks):
    - accuracy of notes and rhythms
    - fluency of performance
    - overall shape and direction of the music.
- Technical control (25 marks):
    - your skill in the techniques of your instrument, voice or technology
    - choice of appropriate tempo
    - level of difficulty of the pieces.
- Realisation of performance markings and/or performance conventions (25 marks):
    - articulation, phrasing and dynamics
    - stylistic conventions, such as ornamentation (for example in baroque music), improvisation (for example in jazz)
    - aural awareness, for example balance, ensemble skills.

Sample examiner's comments

Compare the comments in the following table to see how the examiner responds to a Grade A recital (Learner A) and a Grade E recital (Learner B).

Performing A/Performing B (Section 1)

Criteria	Learner A	Learner B
Knowledge and fluency (25 marks)	An effective performance of both pieces. The notes were accurate, with only a few errors, not enough to lose the flow of the music. The scale passages were neatly done, with a good overall grasp of the shape of the music. **20 marks**	Some knowledge of the notes, promising at times, better in the slow introduction of Piece 1. Some attempt at shaping the music, but too many mistakes in the faster sections, tends to lose fluency. **10 marks**
Technical control (25 marks)	There is a good grasp of technique. The tone was varied to suit the mood of the music. The left hand was accurate and controlled, a variety of bowing techniques were used, with some effective playing in staccato passages. The tempi were well-chosen. **20 marks**	Some control of the instrument, but tone is uneven and breath control needs to be improved. The tempo is rather slow in the faster pieces. The pieces are below Grade 6, so the top two bands of marks are not available. **10 marks**
Realisation of performance markings and/or performance conventions (25 marks)	Most of the expression and ornaments were observed, showing a clear sense of style. Effective contrasts in dynamics made the performances exciting in places. There was good coordination with the accompanist in the transition between fast and slow sections. **20 marks**	Some dynamics and expression are observed at the beginning, but rather careless with these later in the recital, e.g. passages played mezzo forte without any attention to hairpin dynamics. Works quite well with the rest of the group, not always careful to play quietly when needed. **10 marks**
Total marks	**Grade A 60 marks**	**Grade E 30 marks**

Performing B Section 2: Focused study

You are expected to show:

- Interpretative understanding (15 marks):
  - your knowledge of your instrument, voice or technology and your ability to play the type of music which suits it
  - suitable decisions regarding interpretation and technique.
- Stylistic and aural awareness (15 marks):
  - communicate the style and intentions of the original music
  - control and sensitivity of your own performance, and (if in an ensemble) in relation to the other performers.

Sample examiner's comments

Compare the comments to see how the examiner responds to a Grade A recital (Learner A) and a Grade E recital (Learner B).

Criteria	Learner A	Learner B
Interpretative understanding (15 marks)	Effective performance, a few minor errors. Uses staccato accents well to capture comedy style. Good contrast between rhythmic figures and legato phrases, controlled changes from high to low registers. **12 marks**	Some understanding of the voice in blues idiom, but inconsistent in style. Slides and blues intonation not always convincing, lacks confidence in tone and expression. **6 marks**
Stylistic and aural awareness (15 marks)	Secure playing, good control of expression and dynamics, mostly stylish, some character in humorous and lyrical passages. Tempo changes used to suggest 'music hall' mood. **12 marks**	Some understanding of blues style. Needs more confidence in the solo role, but some attempt to relate to the band. **6 marks**
Total marks	**Grade A 24 marks**	**Grade E 12 marks**

Composing

About the component

You should discuss with your teacher at school or college whether to choose Composing A (35%) or Composing B (25%). Your choice will depend on your strengths and interests. Do you prefer performing or composing? Which are you more confident about?

- Composing A (35%) consists of Section 1, Section 2 and Section 3. If you choose this, you must also choose Performing A (25%).

- Composing B (25%) consists of Section 1 and Section 2. If you choose this, you must also choose Performing B (35%).

Component	% of marks	Section 1	Section 2	Section 3	Minimum total length
Composing A	35%	OCR set brief. **35 marks**	Learner set brief. **40 marks**	3 pieces (max. 40" each) in one compositional technique. **30 marks**	8 minutes
Composing B	25%			Section 3 only applies to Composing A	4 minutes

Top ten tips for composing

1. Make sure your compositions are long enough

The minimum total length of pieces for Composing A is 8 minutes. The minimum for Composing B is 4 minutes. If your compositions are too short you will be awarded 0 marks.

2. Investigate how composers respond to a commission

The set briefs specify an audience and/or an occasion for which you are composing. Have clear ideas about how your piece will suit the audience or occasion.

3. Listen to a large variety of music

You need to listen in a concentrated way and note down any ideas that arise from your listening. For example, consider the choice of instruments. Which instruments go well together? Which instruments are used at extremes of range and what effect does this have? What structures are used? How does the composer use melody, rhythm and harmony?

4. Research the work of other composers

Especially those in the genre of your chosen brief.

5. Be serious about your composing

This extends to the score (or equivalent) that you give your performers. Accurate and detailed instructions will help them to perform it well.

6. Give your piece an interesting or meaningful title

This could perhaps be one that reflects the expression or technique in your piece. Show your commitment to the composition. Avoid titles that suggest desperation or a lack of effort (for example 'My A Level composition').

7. Don't leave it to the last minute

If possible test your ideas out with performers. Rewrite things if you need to improve it. Leave time to learn and record the final score.

8. Find a suitable acoustic to record in

Use the best recording equipment and someone who knows how to control it. Don't just record your piece on your phone!

9. Record your compositions live if you can

Persuade other musicians to help you – they will enjoy bringing your notes to life! An audience will give the performance a sense of occasion.

10. Music technology may be used or combined with live performers.

Composing to a brief

Section 1: Composing to a set brief

What the examiners are looking for

You are expected to show:

- Response to brief and ideas (15 marks):
  - a creative and musical response to the commission, audience and venue
  - familiarity with the style, sound and technique of the genre
  - quality of ideas, expressive use of the elements, and the overall structure.
- Compositional techniques (10 marks):
  - your skill in using the elements of music, including melody and harmony
  - how you connect and develop your ideas
  - how you combine sounds in textures and write music which suits the medium (instruments, voices or technology).
- Communication (10 marks):
  - accuracy and attention to detail
  - articulation, phrasing and dynamics.

Section 2: Composing to a learner-set brief

There are 5 marks for the brief which you write in Section 2.

A checklist for writing your own brief

- Write your brief before your composition
- Your brief for Section 2 should be similar in style to the Section 1 briefs provided by OCR
- Include the following in your brief:
  - the type of music you are going to compose – its style or structure
  - the venue or event you are composing for, or a commission or stimulus for the composition
  - the instrumentation, voices or music technology which you plan to use.

Sample learner-created briefs

Learner A

Area of Study 6: Innovations in Music 1900 to the present day

Write a short piece for a small chamber group of three to five instruments, including either a piano or harp. Your piece will be performed at the opening of an exhibition at the Barber Institute of Fine Art in Birmingham. The exhibition, 'An American Impressionist in Paris', will show the work of the American artist Mary Cassatt. She worked for much of her life in France and was much influenced by the Impressionists. Your composition will draw on some of the musical language and techniques of French composers of the time (e.g. Debussy, Ravel) to respond to the style of Cassatt's work. Her later paintings were often of 'mother and child' subjects, but any of her paintings may be a stimulus for your music.

Learner B

Area of Study 2: Popular Song: Blues, Jazz, Swing and Big Band

At the request of a local film-maker, you have been asked to compose a song in blues style as a soundtrack for a short film. The film is about the decline of the local cinema, built in 1923, but which is about to be demolished.

Sample Examiner's comments

Compare the comments on compositions from two candidates to see how the examiner responds to a Grade A composition (Learner A) and a Grade E composition (Learner B).

Criteria	Learner A	Learner B
Effectiveness of the learner set brief (5 marks)	A detailed brief, giving a specific occasion and venue, clearly related to artistic stimulus and musical models. Instrumentation is specified. Good opportunities for further research and creation and development of expressive musical ideas in impressionist idiom. **5 marks**	An interesting idea for a brief – a sense of purpose and a suggested style. It lacks detail, needing more guidance than 'song in blues style', for example guidance about the mood/message of the film, explanation of how the music contributes to the film, resources/ instruments available to the composer. **2 marks**
Response to brief and ideas (15 marks)	Effective piece for flute, harp and cello. Slow intro and faster, dance-like section. Evidence of listening to Ravel's Introduction & Allegro, seen in attractive melodic ideas and use of textures to capture light, playful quality of Cassatt's painting of mother and child. **12 marks**	The song shows some knowledge of blues conventions, based on study of Bessie Smith, but very little of her personality. Melody lacks character, too often moving in step, rather dull. Overall structure works, rather repetitive towards the end. Only a limited attempt to vary the expression. **6 marks**

Compositional techniques (10 marks)	Idiomatic writing for flute (for example contrast between high and low registers, rapid scales and decorations), some effective harp passages and use of pizzicato cello. Secure control of melody and rhythm, develops ideas and uses contrasting themes. Able to change keys and use a variety of harmony (for example passages of parallel seventh chords). **8 marks**	Satisfactory writing for voice and instruments, some errors with text-setting, limited use of blues decoration in melody or accompaniment, mostly basic harmony (for example no sevenths, limited variation of basic chord pattern). More development of motifs and contrast/ variety of material needed. **4 marks**
Communication (10 marks)	Effective and expressive flute part, articulation and dynamics are clear in the recording and in the score. Less detail in harp and cello playing, but the score has appropriate accents and dynamics in the dance section. **7 marks**	Some articulation and dynamics are marked in the score, but they are applied inconsistently. The singer lacks confidence in blues style, with slides and blues expression not fully observed. **4 marks**
Total marks	Grade A 32 marks	Grade E 16 marks

Section 3: Composing A only

Section 3 requires you to compose three short pieces using compositional techniques from an Area of Study from the syllabus.

Tips for Section 3 pieces

- All three pieces must be in the same style. The aim of the exercises is to explore **one** compositional technique
- The exercises must be based on **one** of the Areas of Study – see the examples below

- Relate the style you have chosen to examples of music from the Area of Study. Listen to the music, research the techniques used, discuss these with your teacher

- Make a list of what you find (for example names of different chords, research of rhythmic techniques, examples of textures and how they are created)

- There must be a recording of the pieces. You can perform these yourself, use music technology or have someone else perform them

- There must be a score or a lead sheet or you must describe the music

- Write a brief report on the pieces to make clear the techniques you are exploring. This will help the examiner understand the purpose of the exercises.

Examples of exercises

Choose one Area of Study and one technique to explore in your three maximum-40-second exercises.

Area of Study	Technique Choose either (i) *Pitch organisation,* or (ii) *Rhythm and Metre,* or (iii) *Textures*
AoS 1 **Instrumental Music of Haydn, Mozart and Beethoven**	*Pitch organisation:* Harmony in rondo movements by Mozart *Textures:* Haydn's string quartet writing
AoS 2 Popular Song: Blues, Jazz, Swing and Big Band	*Pitch organisation:* Harmony in Gershwin's songs *Textures:* Techniques in song arrangements by Nelson Riddle
AoS 3 Developments in Instrumental Jazz 1910 to the present day	*Pitch organisation:* Modal jazz (Miles Davis, Herbie Hancock) *Rhythm and Metre:* Swing and syncopation in Count Basie *Textures:* Piano trio arrangements in the style of Bill Evans

AoS 4 **Religious Music of the Baroque Period**	*Pitch organisation:* Chorale harmonisation in the style of J.S. Bach *Textures:* Choral textures in Handel's choruses
AoS 5 **Programme Music 1820–1910**	*Pitch organisation:* Harmonic language of Grieg's Lyric Pieces *Textures:* Tchaikovsky's orchestral writing
AoS 6 **Innovations in Music 1900 to the present day**	*Pitch organisation:* Modal or octatonic techniques *Rhythm and Metre:* Bartók's piano pieces in Bulgarian rhythm *Textures:* contemporary English/American choral music

What the examiners are looking for

You are expected to show:

- Language (10 marks):
  - understanding of pitch, rhythm and texture in the chosen style
  - idiomatic writing for instrument or voice.
- Technique (10 marks):
  - how you use composing techniques and devices to create, connect and develop your ideas
  - how you structure and control the material.
- Compositional coherence (10 marks):
  - how you combine techniques and ideas
  - your use of the medium to make a satisfying piece.

Sample examiner's comments

Compare the comments on compositions from two candidates to see how the examiner responds to a Grade A composition (Learner A) and a Grade E composition (Learner B).

Criteria	Learner A	Learner B
Language (10 marks)	Secure knowledge of harmony in AoS 4 Bach chorale exercises. Clear cadences in correct keys, strong harmony based mostly on primary chords, good identification of modulations. Mostly idiomatic part-writing in the correct vocal ranges. **8 marks**	Some attempt to use the textures in AoS 3 Bill Evans trio style. Some success with Evans' piano style, clear melody, left hand chords. Walking bass is used, not always varied enough for this repertoire. Variety in the use of cymbals, but repetitive rhythms don't match the piano. **4 marks**
Technique (10 marks)	Able to use a variety of harmonies across the 3 exercises, sensible use of inversions, confident use of ii7b–V–I. Passing notes/dissonances are handled effectively. A few errors with parallel 5ths/8ves, but mostly secure. **8 marks**	A few examples of close harmonies and rich chords, some quartal harmonies and parallel movement. Limited awareness of bass and drums, basic textures (for example not exploiting high register of bass). **4 marks**
Compositional coherence (10 marks)	Mostly effective and convincing chorale writing. Bass is usually strong, with a clear sense of direction. Also examples of idiomatic tenor writing, stylish and interesting to sing. Some attention given to the words by using chromatic writing in passion chorale. **8 marks**	Limited understanding of the medium, inconsistent in style, closer to earlier jazz at times. Some effective moments of piano melody and chord voicing, but limited by lack of clear direction in bass and drums. **4 marks**
Total marks	**Grade A 24 marks**	**Grade E 12 marks**

Listening and appraising

About the component

The listening and appraising examination is a written paper taken at the end of the course. The exam lasts 2½ hours. OCR will provide:

- **Question paper.** This contains all the questions and space for you to answer each one. You must write all your answers in the question paper. The question paper with your answers is returned to the exam board for marking.

- **Insert.** A booklet of scores/notated music needed to answer the questions. Each piece of music in the exam is known as an extract: Extract 1, Extract 2, and so on. You can make rough notes on the insert but your final answer must go in the question paper. Examiners will *not* see what you write in the insert.

- **CD.** A recording of the extracts for each question. There will be a short spoken introduction to identify the title and year of the examination. There may be five or six tracks of music, probably 10–15 minutes in total. You will have your own copy of the CD. You will need a CD player and headphones (or other suitable equipment) to listen to it. Your school or college will tell you the arrangements for playback equipment. If you have to provide your own, make sure your equipment has:

  - rewind and fast forward functions. You will want to find some passages quickly and play them over a few times

  - time display in minutes and seconds. The Question Paper may refer to places in the music by timing (for example Explain how the accompaniment changes at 2'45"). You can use the timings to find passages you want to listen to again

  - fresh batteries.

The question paper has blank lined pages for the Section C essays. You should also use these pages if you run out of space answering questions in Sections A and B. Number and letter the question you are answering, for example '1(d)', or '3a'. Ask for more paper if you need it. Write your name and candidate number clearly.

The question paper also includes a music manuscript page for music examples.

> The full specification for your A Level, along with sample papers and mark schemes, can be found on OCR's website, here: www.ocr.org.uk/qualifications/as-a-level-gce-music-h143-h543-from-2016/

Sections of the paper

Section A	Unprepared listening	30 marks
Two extracts: Areas of Study 1 and 2		
Section B	Prescribed works	40 marks
Two extracts: Areas of Study 1 and 2		
Section C	Essays	50 marks

Your two essays must be from different Areas of Study: Areas of Study 3-6. There are eight questions to choose from, two for each Area of Study.

Top tips for the exam

- Revise thoroughly. The exam tests work you should have done over two years of study

- Keep a record in your folder of all the music you have listened to for each Area of Study. Write down key points for each one: title, name of composer, date of composition, bullet points of important details (for example about the music or context)

- Look at the Area of Study pages in the OCR specification. Work out how you would answer questions on each bullet point. See the list of *Topics for you to research and revise* in the tables on pages 63–69

- Read the questions carefully – at least twice! Make sure that you understand the question. Look at the 'command words' – Comment, Explain, Evaluate, Compare. Check if the question has clear instructions about the passage such as 'from bar 21 to bar 28', or 'refer to two or more examples'

- Divide up your time in the exam so that you have enough to answer all the questions: plan how much time you need to answer the two essay questions at the end. Check the clock. When do you need to finish Section B so that you can start Section C?

- Don't get bogged down in Section A questions. If you get stuck, leave it and come back to the question at the end

- If you're in a hurry you can bullet point your answers for longer questions in Section A and Section B

- Section C must be written in essay format, in paragraphs and full sentences.

Section A:
The listening questions

The two extracts for Section A will be of music that you have not prepared for the exam. You may be very lucky and get music you know well, but usually it is music which is unfamiliar.

Question 1 (Extract 1) and Question 2 (Extract 2) will be on music from two Areas of Study:

- Area of Study 1: Instrumental Music of Haydn, Mozart and Beethoven
- Area of Study 2: Popular Song: Blues, Jazz, Swing and Big Band

There are 15 marks for each question (total of 30 marks for Section A).

- Question 1: usually shorter questions, including one word answers
- Question 2: three or four slightly longer questions
- The first extract on the exam paper can be from either Area of Study 1 or 2. If Question 1 is a song (AoS 2), Question 2 will be an extract from Haydn, Mozart or Beethoven (AoS 1)
- The format can vary. It can be the same as last year's or different. Longer questions can appear in Question 1 or shorter questions in Question 2
- Treble clef or bass clef dictation questions can appear in either question.

Listening and making notes

Get into the habit of making notes on your listening in a diary or a log book. This will help you revise for the exam.

What you should know for Section A

Some of your knowledge of Areas of Study 1 and 2 will come from studying the prescribed works for Section B. You should also listen to other music from these periods and have a wider understanding of the background:

Haydn, Mozart, Beethoven

- Dates, where they worked, how their careers overlapped
- How their style of music changed over time
- The orchestra, chamber music, solo performers

- Music in Vienna, London and elsewhere
- The role of patrons and publishers.

Blues, Jazz, Swing, Big Band

- How popular music developed in the 1920s and 1930s
- The role of the solo singer in the 1940s, 1950s
- Later approaches to blues and jazz: 1960s to the present day
- The role of publishers, record companies and radio.

Listen to some typical music from both Areas of Study. Make notes and have a list of music and songs ready for a 'compare' question, for example:

- How is the music extract similar to other music from the period?
- How is this music different to other music (e.g. earlier or later in the period)?

It is easier to answer these if you know the music well.

My listening list for Haydn, Mozart & Beethoven

Genre	Composer/work/date
Solo	Haydn: Piano Sonata in C, Hob. XVI/48 (1789)
	Beethoven: Piano Sonata in C, Op.53, Waldstein (1804)
Chamber music	Haydn: String Quartet in B♭, Op. 76 No. 4, 'Sunrise' (1796–7)
	Beethoven: String Quartet in B♭, Op. 130 (1825)
Concerto	Mozart: Piano Concerto No. 20 in D minor, K.466 (1785)
	Beethoven: Violin Concerto in D, Op. 61 (1806)
Symphony	Haydn: Symphony No. 49 in F minor, Hob. I/49, 'La passione' (1768)
	Haydn: Symphony No. 99 in E♭, Hob. I/99 (1794)
	Beethoven: Symphony No. 7 in A, Op. 92 (1812)
Dramatic music	Mozart: *The Magic Flute*, K.620 – overture (1791)
	Beethoven: Egmont, Op. 84 – overture (1810)
Dance, occasional pieces, variations	Mozart: Serenade for 13 wind instruments (Gran partita) in B♭, K.361 (1781)
	Beethoven: Diabelli Variations, Op. 120 (1819–23)

You don't have to listen to and make notes on all the movements in each work. Spread your listening between the three composers (early, middle and late Classical period). Also have a variety of speeds and structures – first movement forms, rondo, variation, slow movements, minuets and scherzos.

You should go into more detail on some of the music and its background. Highlight some examples to include in answering a comparison question.

Example notes for Area of Study 1

Beethoven: Violin Concerto in D, Op. 61 (1806), first movement	
Style of the music, how it changed over time	*Lyrical, melodic expressive solo part. Avoids double-stopping.* *Important role for woodwind, used as an independent section* *Wide range of dynamics, powerful ff in full orchestra, sfz accents, contrasts with soft/dolce passages* *Very long, 535 bars* *Surprise use of tonality, e.g. entry of full orchestra in Bb major at bar 28.*
The orchestra, chamber music, solo performers	*Double woodwind, brass, timpani (for example opening bar, solo)* *Themes introduced in the woodwind (for example first and second subjects, in harmony, lyrical/diatonic)* *Written for violinist Franz Clement. Beethoven admired his lyrical playing* *Wide range, up to E (2 octaves above open E string). Cadenza – to be improvised by soloist. Coda (2nd subject theme, bar 511), solo marked 'sul D e G' – richer tone of lower strings.*
Performances in Vienna, London and elsewhere	*First performed Theater an der Wien, 23 December 1806* *Benefit concert for Clement (orchestra gave their services for free to help a colleague).*

Patrons, commissions and publishers	*Dedicated to his friend Stephan von Breuning (unusual – not an aristocratic patron)* *Arranged as a piano concerto, dedicated to von Breuning's wife, Julie. Sold for publication to Clementi of London as a separate work Op.61a – more money for Beethoven.*
Themes	*Opening theme, first subject (bars 1–5)*  *Second subject (bars 43–46)*  *First subject in solo violin (bars 101–105)* 
Links (recording, score)	Add a link to a performance, (for example on YouTube) and to an online score (for example from IMSLP).

The Petrucci Music Library is an online resource containing scores and recordings for a vast array of 'public domain' musical works which are out of copyright. You can search for the scores of all of your AoS 1 works here: http://imslp.org

My listening list for Popular Song

Your starting point for AoS 2 should be the prescribed songs for Section B. Choose at least two performances of each song by another singer. If possible include early singers (for example from the 1920s and 1930s) and more recent singers (for example from the 1980s to the present day).

2018 Prescribed work:
Ella Fitzgerald: *The Cole Porter Songbook*, Book 1 (1956)

Song	Singer/date
'Anything goes'	Frank Sinatra (1956) Elaine Page (2007)
'Too darn hot'	Mel Tormé (1960) Sara Gazarek (2006)
'Let's do it'	Unknown singer with B.A. Rolfe & Lucky Strike Orchestra (1929–30) Eydie Gormé (1958) Diana Ross (1971–72)
'Ev'ry time we say goodbye'	Dinah Washington (1956) Cheryl Bentyne (2012)

2019 Prescribed work:
Frank Sinatra: *Classic Sinatra 1953–1960*

Song	Singer/date
'I've got the world on a string'	Ivie Anderson (1933) Diana Krall (1995)
'They can't take that away from me'	Billie Holiday (1937) Steve Tyrell (2003)

| 'I've got you under my skin' | Anita O'Day (1959) Gloria Gaynor (1976) |
| 'Come fly with me' | Shirley Horn (1989) Lou Rawls (2003) |

After this, you will need to fill in the gaps. For example:

- The Blues Queens (for example Bessie Smith)
- Examples of Fred Astaire, Billie Holiday and Bing Crosby
- Early blues artists (for example T-Bone Walker)
- Later blues artists (for example B. B. King)
- Other contemporary singers in jazz (for example Cécile McLorin Salvant, Jamie Cullum) or swing/big band (for example Michael Bublé).

Some songs may need a more detailed chart, with useful examples and comparisons:

Example notes for Area of Study 2

'Let's Face the Music and Dance', sung by Fred Astaire Words and music by Irving Berlin (1935)

| Style of popular song, how it changed over time | Regular two-beat pulse, for dancing
Alternating major and minor (for example C minor – 'There may be trouble ahead', change to C major – 'Let's face the music and dance'). |
| Vocal style | Light voice, clear tone and diction. Relaxed, unforced, higher B section in light, 'floated' tone
Slides between notes, sustained notes, little vibrato, some ornaments (for example mordents), gentle feeling of swing/rhythmic displacement. |

Accompaniment and arrangement	*Film-style orchestra, dominated by strings.* *Violins double the melody* *Brunswick recording sings once through the song, then an extended instrumental section, piano solo for Johnny Green. Film version includes long dance break for Astaire and partner Ginger Rogers.*
Recording, publishers, background	*Written for Hollywood musical Follow the Fleet – Fred Astaire/Ginger Rogers* *Studio recording, 3 mins, made later (1936) for Brunswick Records with Johnny Green & His Orchestra.*
Examples	*Irregular AABA structure, 56 bars* *A1 is 14 bars, opening 4-bar phrase extended by sequence ('moonlight and music and love and romance' = 6 bars)* *Short B section, 8 bars.*
Links (recording, lead sheet)	Add a link to a performance, (for example from YouTube) and to a score/lead sheet (for example from online publishers).

Writing answers in the exam

Tips for answering Section A questions

- Follow the instructions in the question. If it says 'Name one instrument' (for example, clarinet = 1 mark), then don't name two (clarinet, flute = 0 marks). A section is not an instrument (woodwind = 0 marks)

- You can listen to the recording on the CD as often as you like. Use fast-forward/rewind to skip between sections you don't need to listen to again. Make a note of timings, for example on the insert, to help you find important passages

- Practise answering Section A questions. Use past papers and the Rhinegold Education Listening Tests. How much time should you allow for Section A? How many times should you play the music without running out of time?

- Be aware there may be differences between the recording of the song and the lead sheet (see the section entitled 'Lead sheets for songs' on page 38)

- Short, note-style answers are fine in Section A. You don't need long sentences. Use the answer space wisely. If you have big handwriting, make it a bit smaller or be prepared to go on to the additional answer pages in the back

- Describe the music accurately. Use technical language to show you understand the music (for example modulation, diminished 7th, anacrusis)

- Be aware of questions which ask you for an opinion. Your explanation should be rooted in the music or the performance.

  - Example: 'The singer's detached, unemotional singing effectively matches the hopelessness of the words, for example in the lack of vibrato and the dull tone in bar 5'.

- Take care with negative opinions. Give a musical reason

  - Example: 'I don't like the treatment of bar 5 because the lack of vibrato and dull tone makes the performance lifeless'

  - Avoid general statements such as 'The performance is dull and lifeless' or 'I don't like the singer'.

- Identify evidence by the exact place in the music

  - Bar numbers (for example bar 1, bars 45–52)

  - Beat numbers when you need to be precise. The exam paper will use superscript to show the beat number. Bar 3^4 is the 4th beat of bar 3

  - Describe the location (for example the second verse, after the repeat, the bridge section)

  - A timing from the CD (for example 1'42").

Structure

You should be familiar with common structures:

AoS 1 **Instrumental Music of Haydn, Mozart and Beethoven**	Sonata form Rondo form Minuet/scherzo and trio Theme and Variation
AoS 2 Popular Song: Blues, Jazz, Swing and Big Band	32-bar popular song form (AABA) Blues, 12-bar and 8-bar

Answering a question about structure

Using ABC to describe structure

This is a common way to outline the structure of a piece or passage of music. There are no fixed rules for this. Use the letters to tell the examiner what you know.

- Most extracts will be in sections of 8 or 16 bars. Check if the passage divides neatly into sections of roughly equal size. Give one letter to each section. Example: 32-bar song form divides into four sections of 8 bars each: AABA
- You can add numbers to the letters to show different treatment of the same material: AA_1BA_2
- Keep it as simple as possible. If it's too complicated, simplify it (for example 4 or 6 letters) – or write an explanation in sentences
- Watch out for introductions and codas/outros. The first main theme should be A. Don't give an intro a letter: ABBCB is confusing. Instead, write: Intro AABA.

Example question:

> Explain the structure of Cole Porter's song *I Get A Kick Out Of You*
> **[4 marks]**

Mark scheme (the marks that would be given for each of these possible answers appear in brackets):

- AA_1BA_2 (2), Intro–AA_1BA_2 (3)
- AABA (1)
- 64-bar song form, in equal sections of 16 bars (1)
- Introduction (1), with specific detail, for example 4 bars of instrumental, 20 bars of sung introduction: 'My story is much too sad to be told' (1)
- Varied treatment of A melody each time: A, A_1, A_2 (1)
- B section made up of two 8-bar phrases: bb_1 (1)

Some sample answers:

> There is an introduction. At bar 25 the main melody starts, it repeats a few times. It is ABA shape.

Examiner's comment: A weak answer. The introduction is correctly recognised and that it is 24 bars. There is some understanding that the main melody (A) is repeated, but this is a standard AABA form: ABA is too vague to get a mark.

1 mark

> AABA with an introduction. The song is 88 bars in length. The A melody is varied each time.

Examiner's comment: Some accurate information. AABA is correct, also that the A melody is varied. There is no detail about the introduction.

2 marks

> The structure of the main song is 64-bar song form in four 16-bar phrases. The opening 16 bars is repeated but altered to match the lyrics. The B section is two repeated phrases, 8 bars each, changing key at the end to go back to the tonic. The A section returns at the end. The long introduction is typical of songs of this period.

Examiner's comment: Good answer. 64-bar AABA form is described accurately, also the introduction. Aware that the melody changes in both A and B sections.

4 marks

Melodic and bass dictation

At least one question will ask you to complete a few bars of notation from listening to the recording. The score will have a few bars left blank. You can listen to the passage as many times as you like. The rhythm may be printed above the stave, leaving you to work out the missing pitches.

Work out a rough answer on the insert – the examiner will not see this. Copy your finished answer to the stave in the question paper so that it can be marked.

Dictation questions vary from year to year. There may be two questions, one on a melody in treble clef and one on a bass in bass clef. Or there may be only a question on one clef. You should not assume that treble clef will always come up or that the rhythm will always be provided. Be prepared to answer on bass clef or to notate the rhythm.

Top tips for dictation:

- Not everyone learns music through staff notation. Perhaps you picked up music mostly by ear or through tab notation. Learning staff notation takes some practice. Don't leave it to the last minute. Sing and hum melodies and basses in your head. Practise singing and playing from notation. Do this throughout the course

- Dictation is marked by intervals, the steps and leaps between the notes (see the example below)

- Revise the intervals in major and minor scales so that you know the sound of major 2nd, minor/major 3rd, perfect 4th, perfect 5th, minor/major 6th, minor/major 7th, and octave

- Get used to the sound of chromatic notes – sharps, flats and naturals. They often sound out of place in a diatonic scale. Practise recognising them

- In the exam, hum the melody or bass in your head. Play the bars a few times so that you can remember it. Check what you write by humming note by note

- Check your answer against the chords/harmony. Does your melody fit against the bass?

- Don't change the rhythm if it's provided. There should be one pitch for each note. Watch out for tied notes, which will look like two notes tied together with a curved line but will sound like one note

- If you can't work it all out, don't leave gaps and guess the notes. Show how the melody goes up and down, whether it moves by step, where the leaps are. There may be 1 mark for the general shape even if the detail is not correct.

An example: In the following dictation example, from Beethoven's 'Eroica' Symphony, 2nd movement, only the melody in the first two bars was provided.

Mark scheme: Dictation is marked by interval. This means that each interval between notes that you identify correctly is 'right' even if because of an earlier mistake, you are now on the wrong notes of the staff. The correct answer scores 4 marks. 1 or 2 errors score 3 marks; 3 or 4 errors score 2 marks; 1 mark would be awarded for a general shape which is correct.

Correct answer (4 marks):

Student answer (2 marks):

This answer has three errors, marked with an X. The two errors in intervals are marked with brackets. The final X is a wrong note between two correct ones. This answer therefore scores 2 marks.

Writing about performances

Section A may include questions about the performances or the recordings you are listening to. Studying the prescribed works for Section B (see page 39 onwards) should give you plenty of experience of writing about performances.

You should know about:

- Performing conventions in Haydn, Mozart and Beethoven (such as ornaments, repeats, cadenza)

- The different sound of 'period' instruments compared to 'modern' instruments. For example, in Haydn's day stringed instruments had a shorter neck, a shorter bow and gut strings. Modern string instruments have a fuller tone and more ability to sustain notes and phrases. Compare also the construction and sound of the piano, woodwind, brass and timpani

- The poorer sound of older recordings (for example from the 1920s and 1930s) and the performance practice of the time. Microphones and studio technology were limited. The bass or inner parts can be difficult to hear, while the melody can be bright or harsh.

Lead sheets for songs

You should be aware that there may be important differences between the two versions of the song in Section A – the one recorded on the CD and the printed lead sheet in the insert.

The lead sheet is the published version of the song. Often this is the closest to what the composer intended – but not always. Sometimes publishers make changes to a song. This may include changing the structure, cutting/ extending or repeating sections. When a recording is made the arranger may make more changes, perhaps altering the tempo and style of the song to suit the singer and band in the recording. Changes in harmony may be made. The singer will want the song in a key that suits his/her voice. High sections or low sections may be sung in a different way to show off the best parts of the voice. Finally, the singer can change rhythms and pitches quite freely.

Performers of Haydn, Mozart and Beethoven usually take the composer's intentions very seriously. Compare the CD and insert in sample or past papers from A Level and AS Level to see what can happen in Popular Song performances. Changes between the published song and the recording are not 'errors' or 'mistakes'. You may be asked to identify the differences between the lead sheet and the recording.

Historical context

There may be questions about the context of the music, for example:

- Compare the style of the extract to earlier or later music in the period

- Estimate a date for the music

- Comment on the purpose of the music, how or where the music would have been played or sung

- Write about the first audiences, how they would have heard the music, what they would have expected

- Discuss performance or recording conditions, including instruments and technology.

Section B:
Prescribed works

The extracts for Section B will be from music that you have studied for the examination, known as 'prescribed works' (sometimes called 'set works').

The prescribed works change every year. Make sure that you are learning the correct ones:

Area of Study 1: Instrumental Music of Haydn, Mozart and Beethoven

2018   Beethoven: Symphony No. 3 in E♭, Op. 55, 'Eroica', 1st movement

2019   Mozart: Piano Concerto No. 23 in A, K.488, 3rd movement

Area of Study 2: Popular Song: Blues, Jazz, Swing and Big Band

2018   Ella Fitzgerald: *The Cole Porter Songbook* Bk 1 – (i) 'Anything goes', (ii) 'Too darn hot', (iii) 'Let's do it', (iv) 'Ev'ry time we say goodbye'.

2019   Frank Sinatra: *Classic Sinatra 1953–1960* – (i) 'I've got the world on a string', (ii) 'They can't take that away from me', (iii) 'I've got you under my skin', (iv) 'Come fly with me'.

Scores and recordings

- OCR does not specify which score you should use for Area of Study 1
- A number of useful websites have downloadable scores by Haydn, Mozart and Beethoven, usually in older editions. Also check out more modern scholarly editions, sometimes called Urtext editions
- You must use the correct recordings of the songs in Area of Study 2

You are not allowed the score in the exam. If a score is needed (for example for the Haydn, Mozart or Beethoven prescribed work), it will be provided in the insert. The score extract will be specially prepared for the exam, so it will look different to your edition of the score. Watch out for differences in the layout of the score, the notation, languages (for example English, German, Italian) and bar numbers.

Top tips for studying prescribed works

- Make a copy of the scores to write your study notes on. A large version – A3 size – is easier to see
- Have a spare blank copy available. Test how well you remember your notes
- Hum, sing or whistle the parts – with or without the recording. This is a good way to get to know the music and the score. Start with Violin 1, then have a go at the bass
- Get copies of the lead sheets or piano/vocal/guitar copies for the songs. Sing, play or make your own arrangements
- Listen to different performances of the music, including 'period' and historical performances
- Listen to different arrangements of the songs. Make notes to revise different versions
- Research the background: composers, publishers, record companies, the first audiences.

Questions in Section B

There are four questions on the prescribed works, each worth 10 marks. You must answer:

- Both Questions 3(a) and 3(b) on Area of Study 1

AND

- Both Questions 4(a) and 4(b) on Area of Study 2

Total for Section B: 40 marks

Each question has a page of lines for your answer. You can continue answers on the additional pages.

Insert and CD

The contents of the insert and the CD may vary, but you will probably find:

Prescribed works	CD	Insert
Extract 3 **2018** Beethoven: Symphony No. 3 'Eroica' **2019** Mozart: Piano Concerto No. 23	A short passage from the prescribed movement **There may be:** A second performance of the extract (for you to compare the versions)	A full score of the extract

Extract 4

2018 Ella Fitzgerald

2019 Frank Sinatra

One of the songs sung by the prescribed singer or by a different singer

There may be:

Two performances of the song (for you to compare the versions)

There may be:

A lead sheet for the song extract

What you need to know:

	Question 3(a) and (b) Area of Study 1	Question 4(a) and (b) Area of Study 2
Analysis	Write about: ■ Instruments and how they are used, texture ■ How melodies and themes are used ■ Harmony, chords, cadences, tonality, modulations ■ Dynamics and expression ■ Structure.	Write about: ■ The voice, vocal technique of the singer ■ How the melody is shaped to express the lyrics ■ Harmony, chords, chord symbols, cadences, tonality, modulations ■ Interpretation of the song: dynamics, expression, delivery of the lyrics ■ Structure of the song, decisions by the arranger about structure ■ The accompaniment, instruments and how they are used, relationship with the voice (such as to bring out the meaning of the words).

Comparison	**Write about:**	**Write about:**
	▪ Different performances: period instruments, modern instruments, historical recording	▪ Different performances, for example compare with another singer
	▪ Interpretation, for example tempo, articulation, phrasing, dynamics and expressive decisions by performers	▪ Interpretation of the song, for example tempo, beat, vocal style, expression, delivery of the words, arrangement, accompaniment
	▪ Compare two extracts on the CD	▪ Compare two extracts on the CD
	▪ Compare performances you have studied.	▪ Compare performances you have studied.
Context	**Write about:**	**Write about:**
	▪ Background to the work and its composer, such as when and why it was created	▪ Background to the song and the singer, such as when and why it was recorded
	▪ Performance practice at the time, working conditions for musicians, commissions and money, printing and publication, audiences	▪ Background to its composer and arranger, such as when and why it was created
	▪ Comparison to other music in this Area of Study, for example works in this genre by Haydn, Mozart or Beethoven; earlier or later works by this composer	▪ Performance practice, working conditions for musicians, studio and live recording, recording technology, radio and TV, contracts and money, publishing, audiences
	▪ Notation of the score, different editions.	▪ Comparison to other music in this Area of Study, for example other recorded songs in this genre; earlier or later recordings by this singer.

Sample answers on prescribed works

This section contains some examples of answers to questions on prescribed works.

Read the answers on your prescribed works carefully. They show the style of writing and how much detail are needed. The 'Examiner's comments' show what an examiner might think of the answer – and how many marks it might get.

The following table shows the type of answers covered in this section. You will find it helpful to read the answers for the works you are not studying, as they are clear examples of the level of knowledge and detail that will be required of you in those you are.

Year	Prescribed work	Analysis	Comparison	Context
2018	Beethoven 'Eroica' Symphony	Example B1 Thematic material	Example B5 Two modern performances	Example B9 Development of the symphony
	Fitzgerald *Cole Porter Songbook*	Example B2 Melody and lyrics	Example B6 Fitzgerald and one other	Example B10 Career as a singer
2019	Mozart Piano Concerto No. 23	Example B3 Writing for piano	Example B7 Modern and period performance	Example B11 Making a living as a performer-composer
	Sinatra 1950s recordings for Capitol	Example B4 Harmony	Example B8 Sinatra and one other	Example B12 Role of record companies

Mark scheme

All questions are marked out of 10. The mark scheme will be different for each question and for each prescribed work. There will be common features, for example:

SAMPLE ANSWERS ON PRESCRIBED WORKS

9–10 marks	Precise and detailed answer. Perceptive, accurate technical terms. Consistent examples of listening, locations/bar numbers.
7–8 marks	Clear and detailed. Good understanding, relevant technical terms. Relevant examples.
5–6 marks	Relevant, with some detail. General understanding, some technical terms. Some examples.
3–4 marks	Partly accurate and relevant answer. Some understanding, not always accurate. A few examples, not always relevant.
1–2 marks	Weak answer. Limited understanding. Little use of examples.
0 marks	No accurate or relevant comments.

Top tips for Section B answers:

- Revise the prescribed works thoroughly. You may be expected to write about a movement/song from memory (without a score or recording)
- Read the question carefully. Is there a list of what you must write about?
- Make general points (at least 5 or 6 different points) **and** give examples
- Include relevant details:
  - bar numbers or locations (such as 'in the first verse', 'on the word 'love'')
  - names of performers, concert venues, recording studios, producers, arrangers
  - names of chords, keys, instruments
  - dates
  - technical words and musical terms.
- Each question takes up a single page. Use all the lines, if you can
- Small handwriting helps. If you have larger handwriting, continue into the blank space on the page or use the additional lines at the end of the exam paper. Ask for extra paper if you need it
- Check the question again. Have you covered everything?

Analysis questions

These questions will require you to write about the music: the question words will be things like 'comment', 'discuss' and 'describe'. To learn what is required of you, compare the high and low scoring samples answers in the following examples.

Example B1, 2018 – Beethoven: 'Eroica' Symphony

Materials provided: Score and audio, bars 322–398[1].

Comment on the treatment of thematic material at the end of the development (bars 322–398[1]). Refer to bar numbers in your answer. **[10 marks]**

Sample student answer:

The passage begins with the development theme (not heard in the exposition). It is in two-bar phrases in the key of Eb minor, played in close harmony by the clarinets, bassoons and cellos. It modulates to Gb major at bar 330. The two-bar phrase is passed between the violins (the first time with flute) and cellos, this time without the close harmony. A new section starts at bar 338 based on the opening theme of the movement, played in chords by the woodwind and horns, with a rich texture of overlapping repetitions of the theme. The ascending staccato crotchets in broken chords in the violas, cellos and basses are based on the accompaniment to the transition theme (bar 45). The development ends with repeated chords in the woodwind and horns. The strings answer with an ascending triad (bar 369), a motif from the opening theme. The harmony is varied and the rhythm changed into quavers. The suspense at the end of the development is interrupted by the false entry of the opening theme (bars 394–395) by the solo horn, anticipating the recapitulation which follows.

Examiner's comments:

- Able to explain the thematic material, for example knows that the bar 322 theme is only in the development. Bar numbers are accurate, there is some detail (the answer refers to tonality and scoring)
- Able to link thematic material to the exposition, explaining where it came from.

Mark awarded: **9/10**

Example B2, 2018 – Ella Fitzgerald: *Cole Porter Songbook*

Materials provided: Audio of the complete song, no score.

Describe the phrasing and structure of the melody in 'Let's do it' and comment on the relationship between melody and lyrics in the song. **[10 marks]**

Sample student answer:

The melody is in AABA 32-bar song form. The three words 'let's do it' provide the rhythm of a three-note motif. The A sections are built up of repetitions of this motif. In the first 8 bars, the motif is repeated in bars 1, 2, 4, 5 and 6. The motif has descending chromatic pitches in Porter's original score and in early recordings at a faster dance tempo, but Fitzgerald (at a slower tempo) varies the motif to maintain interest. She often repeats the first note and descends a step on the third. She also varies the rhythm, for example treating the first note as detached or sustained, and also delaying it until the second beat. The repetition of 'do it' is important in the humour of the lyrics. The first word can be replaced (for example 'birds', 'bees') or a longer phrase (for example 'the best upper sets') with 'do it' added at the end.

Examiner's comments:

- Overall understanding of the AABA structure

- Careful and detailed explanation of the 'let's do it' motif, with examples of lyrics and reference to bar numbers. Perceptive comment on Fitzgerald's interpretation of the song and how she varies the motif
- Most of the comment is about the beginning of the song. No explanation of how the B section is structured or how the motif goes higher to end the song.

Mark awarded: 7/10

Example B3, 2019 – Mozart: Piano Concerto No. 23

Materials provided: No score, no audio.

Discuss Mozart's writing for piano in this movement. **[10 marks]**

Sample student answer:

This concerto is less virtuosic than his other piano concertos. The writing is highly melodic: ten different themes can be identified in this movement. The rondo theme at the beginning is in the right hand: a three-note motif, detached, followed by two bars of quavers. The left hand is a fast Alberti bass accompaniment in quavers. The next piano theme (from bar 62) moves in crotchets. Mozart uses grace notes and turns to decorate the right hand melody, which has a range of two octaves. The focus is on the lyrical, constantly moving melody. The accompaniment is mostly limited to Alberti bass and chords, often in middle register. Towards the end of the opening section Mozart uses octaves in the left hand, alternating with broken chord figures in quavers in the right hand. Later he swaps the parts around so that the left hand has the intricate quaver broken chords. Mozart's piano would have been lighter in tone than a modern piano, especially in the bass.

Examiner's comments:

- There is good understanding of the writing for piano, including the melodic style of the movement. Some relevant comments on the role of each hand and the relationship between melody and accompaniment

- Good with examples from the beginning of the movement, including an accurate bar number. Less detail from later in the movement, for example scales in 10ths in the Coda

- The 'swap' of the parts is in the first episode/second subject – this location could have been mentioned. In this section the piano part becomes more active and virtuosic, for example leaps of a 12th (B to F), use of the full range of the piano, descending broken octaves in the left hand, leading to a new piano theme (bar 176) over a pedal E Alberti bass.

Mark awarded: **7/10**

Example B4, 2019 – Sinatra: 1950s recordings for Capitol

Materials provided: Audio of the complete song, lead sheet (melody, lyrics and chords).

Outline the characteristic features of the harmony and tonality in Sinatra's recording of 'Come Fly With Me'. **[10 marks]**

Sample student answer:

Sinatra's version of the song is in the key of B major. The introduction has a rising chromatic figure to suggest a plane taking off, ending on a dominant chord (F#13). The melody is harmonised by rich chords, usually extended by adding 7ths or 9ths, with some 6ths, 11ths and 13ths. The walking bass provides a clear direction to the harmony. Chord progressions are often based on secondary dominants, with roots a 4th or 5th apart. For example, in bars 3–8 the movement in the bass is C# – F# – B – E – A. In the A sections (bars 1–16), chords change mostly once a bar. The bridge (B) has a slower harmonic rhythm, with chord changes every two bars, suggesting a 'glide' at high altitude. The tonality of the bridge is G major, which is distant from the tonic, i.e. far from the ground. The harmony returns to the tonic by changing key to the dominant, F# major.

Examiner's comments:

- Very good understanding of the harmony, explaining the rich chords, the role of the walking bass in providing a strong progression and the use of contrast in the bridge.

- A few clear and accurate examples, with bar numbers or references to locations in the lead sheet.

- Possibly should mention chromatic movement (for example change from Bmaj9 to B9, or chromatic phrases in brass close harmony), but overall a very good answer.

Mark awarded: 9/10

Comparison questions

These questions will require you to compare recordings on the CD (or ones which you have chosen).

Top tips for comparison questions:

- Mention **similarities**, but most of all comment on **differences**

- Mention **general** points that apply to the whole recording (for example faster/slower, small orchestra/big orchestra), but most of all write about the **detail** in the music. Be precise with bar numbers, describe what you hear in detail (for example melodies, articulation, phrasing)

- Look out for differences in pitch: period performances often sound a semitone lower but this is not a different key: the music is tuned lower, not transposed

- Explain changes in tempo, including unmarked changes, for example faster or slower compared to the usual pulse

- You may comment on the quality of the recording or studio techniques, such as the balance between instruments, the poor sound of a historical recording. Also issues of the acoustic, such as reverb in a large venue or closeness to/ distance from the microphone

- You can say which performance you prefer. Back up your opinion with evidence from the music

- Two extracts on the CD will be called 3a and 3b (or 4a and 4b). Check that you don't get them mixed up as you write. If you prefer, use the CD track numbers instead

- If you are asked to discuss your own choice of recording, give plenty of detail. Persuade the examiner that you know it well.

Example B5, 2018 – Beethoven: 'Eroica' Symphony

Materials provided: Score and audio, bars 1–45.

Both performances used in this question can be found on YouTube (but there will be no video in the exam – audio CD only):

Extract 3a: Christian Thielmann (conductor), Wiener Philharmoniker. Timing: 1'03"–1'58".

Extract 3b: Nathalie Stutzmann (conductor), Tapiola Sinfonietta. Timing: 0'32"–1'26".

Compare the two performances of bars 1–45, commenting on similarities and differences. You may wish to refer to:

- The orchestra
- Tempo
- Articulation
- Other details of the interpretation. **[10 marks]**

Sample student answer 1:

3a has a bigger orchestra. There is more of an echo because it is a larger concert hall. The orchestra in 3b is smaller and there is a dry acoustic so there is no reverb on the chords at the beginning. Both performances have a similar tempo but 3b gets faster at the end. The articulation is good in the first performance but not so good in 3b. The violins play louder in 3b.

Examiner's comments:

- A good comment on the size of the orchestra, linked to the venue/acoustic with a detail about 3b
- Mostly general comments, superficial, lacks detail. It's not clear if 'articulation' is understood. Very little on interpretation.

Mark awarded: 2/10

Sample student answer 2:

The orchestra in 3a is larger, with a full string section. The opening chords are strongly accented, slightly lengthened to give a feeling of power. The smaller orchestra in 3b is more of a chamber orchestra. The opening chords are very staccato and less powerful but with a feeling of being faster. There is a fast tempo in both. 3a varies the tempo in bar 6 to make the phrase more expressive the cellos have a rit. and a diminuendo before the C♯ then a crescendo is added.

3b is a lighter performance. The sforzandi are less strong because of the smaller orchestra, for example in bars 28–34 the music is quieter with only slight accents, which makes the crescendo in bars 35–36 an effective contrast. In 3a this passage is louder throughout, building up to a very loud *ff* at bar 37. In 3b the small orchestra means that the second violins can be heard more clearly in bars 13 and 15.

Examiner's comments:

- Detailed answer, good comments on overall performance, with examples from places in the score (with bar numbers)
- Good examples of changes in tempo and the way the *sf* markings are performed. Able to explain how the details help the performance (for example 'more expressive', 'effective contrast')
- One more paragraph with this sort of detail would be awarded 9 or 10 marks.

Mark awarded: **7/10**

Example B6, 2018 – Ella Fitzgerald: *The Cole Porter Songbook*

Materials provided: No score, audio (two tracks) of 'Too darn hot'.

Extract 4a: Ella Fitzgerald

Extract 4b: Sammy Davis Jr. (from compilation album *Sammy & Friends*, Rhino UK 1999).

Compare the interpretations of 'Too darn hot' by Ella Fitzgerald and Sammy Davis Jr. Comment on points of interest in both extracts, including the singing style of both performers. **[10 marks]**

Sample student answer:

Fitzgerald's is a longer version, including a whole verse for the band. Davis cuts out the middle verses and repeats the 'Kinsey Report' bridge almost immediately. He fades out at the end (Fitzgerald builds up to a big finish). Both have a similar tempo. Fitzgerald has a walking bass in a crotchet pulse all the way through the song. Davis has a minim pulse at the beginning and only breaks into crotchets at the bridge. The bridge is louder and more swinging (Fitzgerald's band gets quieter). Davis goes into stop time for the 'thermometer' passage – the rhythm section stops and there are detached/accented chords on the first beat of the bar. The rhythmic changes make the Davis version exciting.

Fitzgerald's singing is very stylish and accurate with the melody. She has clear diction and brings out the humour in the words, for example with blue notes and slides. Davis is rougher, more likely to change notes and exaggerate the humour slightly. He sings 'thermometer' to a repeated note the first time. He improvises the repetitions to 'too darn hot', lengthening the 'too' each time. His band features an electric guitar (introduction and fills), suggesting a performance recorded later than Fitzgerald's. His band is louder, more brass dominated, while she has more saxophones playing a two-note motif.

Examiner's comments:

- Effective comparison of the two performances. Manages to comment on the structure, the band and on the style of singing in both performances
- Perceptive comment on the pulse in both songs, explaining how the variety in Davis creates an exciting effect
- Some comment on the singing, slightly general but good specific detail on Davis.

Mark awarded: 9/10

Example B7, 2019 – Mozart: Piano Concerto No. 23

Materials provided: Score and audio.

Listen to two performances of bars 62-105. Both performances are on YouTube (but there will be no video in the exam – audio CD only):

Extract 3a: Ingrid Fliter (piano), BBC Symphony Orchestra. Timing: 19'37"–20'16".

Extract 3b: Malcolm Bilson (piano), English Baroque Soloists. Timing: 18'23"–19'02".

Compare the two performances of bars 62-105. Comment on similarities and differences. You may wish to refer to:

- The interpretation of the piano solo
- The accompaniment
- The overall sound of the instruments
- The recording. **[10 marks]**

Sample student answer 1:

Extract 3b is performed on a fortepiano, 3a on a modern piano. You can hear the dynamics more clearly on the modern piano. Also it is more staccato and legato because the technology is better. 3b is the same volume all the way through.
The accompaniment is on period instruments, which play in a different key. The tempo is the same in both performances.

Examiner's comments:

- Understands basic details of modern and 'period' instruments, but general comments, no evidence of detailed listening.
- Some comments are not clearly explained (e.g. 'more staccato and legato') or confused (e.g. 'play in a different key').

Mark awarded: 3/10

Sample student answer 2:

Extract 3a is a live performance. It is on a modern piano with a strong tone, recorded so that the accompanying strings can hardly be heard. Extract 3b is a piano from Mozart's time, tuned slightly lower, and which has a lighter but penetrating tone. The changes in harmony in the strings are easier to hear in bars 89–97.

In 3a there is a wider variety of dynamics and articulation in the solo passagework. The soloist plays a gradual crescendo in bars 77–80, followed by a diminuendo leading up to the high E in bar 831. There is a contrasting strong arpeggio in the left hand at bar 90, then a long diminuendo over the next 6 bars of the descending sequence. The soloist varies the articulation by playing the first two phrases legato and the final phrases staccato (bars 95–96). In 3b the piano has less sustaining power and there is less contrast between loud and soft. The solo passage in bars 62–69 is more relaxed and expressive for example, the staccato crotchets in bar 64 are lighter and not so heavily accented.

Examiner's comments:

- The performances are well understood. There are good general comments on the pianos, tuning and the recorded sound.
- There is evidence of careful listening in the discussion of dynamics and articulation, especially in bars 77–96 of 3a. Technical language is used accurately and confidently. There are a number of examples, located exactly with bar numbers.
- One more paragraph with this sort of detail would be awarded 9 or 10 marks.

Mark awarded: 7/10

Example B8, 2019 – Sinatra: 1950s recordings for Capitol

Materials provided: No score, audio only.

Sarah Vaughan's recording of 'They can't take that away from me', recorded 1954, re-released on her 1957 album *Swingin' Easy*.

Compare the interpretations of 'They can't take that away from me' by Frank Sinatra and Sarah Vaughan and comment on their effectiveness.
[10 marks]

Sample student answer:

Sinatra has a larger band, Vaughan has only a piano trio. Her version is longer and more jazzy when the song is repeated. Sinatra sings an introduction and once through the AABA structure of the song. Vaughan has no sung introduction but she says/half-sings 'Oh, take me home, take me home once more' over the solo piano intro. She sings the song twice through. She improvises some of the melodies and repeats words (for example 'never' and 'bumpy' are repeated several times, giving the song a playful feel). She sings out of tune on the words 'off key'.

Examiner's comments:

- Some relevant comments on Vaughan, including some detail in structure and interpretation
- Makes a judgement that the repeated words create a playful feel. Notices the interpretation of 'off key' but misses the opportunity to give an opinion about whether this is effective or not
- Brief comment on Sinatra, but very limited in detail (regarding his style of singing, interpretation). Mentions the structure of both, but not much comparison. Sinatra is a prescribed work so there should be detail and a judgement on how effective his performance and arrangement are.

Mark awarded: 5/10

Context questions

In these questions you will be required to write about the background to the music. To learn what is required of you, compare the high and low scoring sample answers in the following examples.

Example B9, 2018 – Beethoven: 'Eroica' Symphony

Materials provided: No score, no audio

Outline the differences between the 'Eroica' Symphony and a symphony by Haydn or Mozart. **[10 marks]**

Sample student answer:

The 'Eroica' Symphony is much larger than a Haydn or Mozart symphony. The smaller scale of Haydn's symphonies allowed him to write them more quickly. The 'Eroica' first movement is twice as long as in earlier symphonies. Haydn's 'Drum Roll' Symphony No. 103 has a slow introduction with the drum roll before the main fast section (he also interrupts the end of the recapitulation with a slow section). Beethoven does not have an introduction and maintains the Allegro con brio pace throughout the movement. The exposition, development and recapitulation sections are longer. The themes are similar in length but extended and developed more. The coda is 140 bars, long compared to Haydn. Beethoven uses tonality to create suspense. For example, he could return to the tonic in bar 316 in the development, but he quickly changes to Eb minor and the return is delayed. The music then makes a long build up, with a dramatic pianissimo and the false entry of the solo horn. At the end of the recapitulation, the long coda is set up by repeating the theme in descending steps of Db major and C major, taking the music away from the tonic Eb major.

Beethoven's symphony was created as a tribute to Napoleon, later changed to 'Sinfonia Eroica'. Many Haydn symphonies have nicknames. These were not his titles but made up later to illustrate moments of the music (e.g. 'Drum Roll', because the symphony begins with a drum roll). 'Eroica' applies to the whole symphony. The slow movement is a funeral march. The third movement is a scherzo – faster, more intense than the Minuet which Haydn would have used.

The orchestra is similar to Haydn's London symphonies – double woodwind, 3 horns (Haydn used 2), 2 trumpets and timpani. Beethoven makes greater use of solo woodwind to exchange motifs. Haydn uses the woodwind more as a section, with little use of solo woodwind (expect to double the strings). Both composers use contrasts in dynamics and articulation, but Beethoven uses ff and sf more. Accents are often reinforced by the full orchestra.

Examiner's comments:

- Good, detailed comments on Beethoven. Aware of the scale of the work compared to earlier symphonies. Specific detail on tonality and structure
- Able to compare with a symphony by Haydn, with examples showing familiarity with the music.

Mark awarded: 9/10

Example B10, 2018 – Ella Fitzgerald: *The Cole Porter Songbook*

Materials provided: No score, no audio

Describe how Ella Fitzgerald's experience as a performer made her the ideal singer to record *The Cole Porter Songbook*. **[10 marks]**

Sample student answer:

Fitzgerald was 38 years old when she recorded The Cole Porter Songbook. By 1956 she had been in the business for over twenty years. She made her first recording in 1935 with the Chick Webb band. Her recording of 'A-Tisket, A-Tasket' sold millions and showed her appeal to both black and white audiences. She led the band for six years when Webb died, leaving in 1942 to concentrate on a solo career. Fitzgerald had an excellent singing technique and maintained the quality of her voice over a long career. A white singer of her quality would have had her own radio show, but she had to work hard at a busy schedule of concerts and guest appearances on the radio. She was used to performing long sets, drawing on her large repertoire of songs. She performed at the Jazz at the Philharmonic concerts for Norman Granz. He took over as her manager and chose her as the ideal singer to record The Cole Porter Songbook for his new record company, Verve. Her accurate pitch and diction, the flexibility of her voice over a wide range and her natural swing style allowed her to sing most songs. She could learn new songs quickly and record unfamiliar numbers with little rehearsal.

Examiner's comments:

- Able to explain Fitzgerald's background and qualities as a singer, with a few detailed examples
- Aware of the professional relationship with manager/producer Norman Granz
- Very good on the background. A more detailed example (for example relating her experience to the singing on one or two tracks of the album) would take this to full marks.

Mark awarded: 8/10

Example B11, 2019 – Mozart: Piano Concerto No. 23

Materials provided: No score, no audio

Explain Mozart's life as a performer-composer in the 1780s. **[10 marks]**

Sample student answer:

Mozart was in Vienna for most of the 1780s. After leaving the service of the Archbishop of Salzburg in 1781, he made a living as a freelance musician, performing his own music, teaching pupils and composing to commissions by wealthy patrons. He worked hard to make a living as a pianist and composer. The piano concertos were an important source of income for Mozart. Between 1782 and 1786 he wrote 15 concertos to play at his subscription concerts. At the same time he was writing other music, for example his opera 'The Marriage of Figaro'. He had 450 gulden from Artaria, the publishers of the string quartets he dedicated to Haydn. The success of his operas and the income from publishing led him to perform less and compose more for publication. He travelled to Prague and to Germany, but a planned visit to London never took place because his father Leopold would not look after Mozart's family while he was away. He took a minor post at the Imperial court to provide dance music, which gave him a small regular income.

Examiner's comments:

- Good overview of Mozart's career in Vienna, showing awareness of his busy life and sources of income
- Some precise detail (such as accurate dates, reference to compositions, details of payment from publisher)
- Makes a variety of points – relevant, interesting and informed.

Mark awarded: 9/10

Example B12, 2019 – Sinatra: 1950s recordings for Capitol

Materials provided: No score, no audio

Explain the role of recording companies in 1950s popular song, referring to the prescribed songs by Frank Sinatra. **[10 marks]**

Sample student answer:

Frank Sinatra recorded for Capitol Records. In the 1950s there was huge competition between record companies. Best-selling records would sell millions of copies. It was important for companies to have contracts with the best singers and to sign new talent. Sinatra recorded a series of albums for Capitol, including Songs for Swingin' Lovers and Come Fly With Me. They were in the new LP format, so lots of songs had to be recorded to fill two sides of 20–30 minutes each. Capitol was based in Hollywood.

Examiner's comments:

- Some general knowledge of the background, a few examples, aware of competition between companies and importance of contracts with singers
- Limited in detail, missed opportunities to mention other singers and record companies. Aware of Sinatra's 1950s albums – but could also mention 'concept album', working with arrangers (Nelson Riddle, Billy May)
- More needed on record companies, for example Capitol's risk in promoting Sinatra (regarded by many as past his best), Alan Livingston's artistic management (aiming for a new sound without 'romantic' strings, matching Sinatra with Riddle). Also radio broadcasts, competition with television, increased sales in new formats (10-inch and 12-inch vinyl LP, 45rpm single, juke box), importance of solo singer in this era (competing with other large markets such as rock'n'roll, jazz).

Mark awarded: 5/10

Section C:
The essay questions

There are no prescribed works for Section C. You and your teacher must choose your own programme of listening for two of Areas of Study 3–6. You can find a note about this, and some suggestions, from page 34 of the A Level specification document on OCR's website.

> The full specification for your A Level, along with sample papers and mark schemes, can be found on OCR's website, here: www.ocr.org.uk/ qualifications/as-a-level-gce-music-h143-h543-from-2016/

Instead of prescribing works for AoS3–6, OCR provides 'focuses for learning' which can be found in the tables printed on pages 9–12 of the A Level specification. Your choice of music should cover those topics.

There are three types of topic:

- **Musical styles**
Each Area of Study is subdivided into different types of music, such as early jazz or bebop, Baroque Anglican or French church music, programme concert overtures or solo piano works, serialism or minimalism

- **Musical elements**
These are aspects of musical language and technique, such as jazz improvisation, recitative and aria, dynamics and expression, sonority and timbre

- **Conditions and context**
This is the background history of the music, the musicians and its audience, for example:

AoS3 – the origins of jazz, Jelly Roll Morton and Louis Armstrong, demand for jazz in Chicago and New York

AoS4 – worship in Lutheran churches in Germany, Bach's duties as Cantor at Leipizig, his relationship with the Leipzig authorities

AoS5 – creation of Berlioz's 'Symphonie fantastique', influence of Beethoven and Shakespeare on Berlioz, Schumann's response to 'Symphonie fantastique'

AoS6 – background to Shostakovich's Symphony No. 5, Shostakovich's fear of arrest, working conditions for Soviet composers.

Listening to music

Your programme of listening for each Area of Study can be your teacher's choice, your personal preferences or a combination of the two. As well as the list of suggested repertoire in the specification, there are other suggestions below.

You should get to know some of these works very well – if possible well enough to be able to recall them in the exam and discuss them in detail.

Top tips:

- Keep a notebook or diary of your exploration of the Area of Study. Make a note of relevant listening, even if you only listen to the music once

- Get a score of the music if you can

- It pays to listen to the music several times. Good music usually gets more interesting and rewarding with repeated listening. Your knowledge and enthusiasm for music you know well will come through in your exam answers

- Link your listening to the styles, elements and/or conditions and context that you need to know about. Use the checklist of elements to check you have covered everything

- The column called 'Topics for you to research and revise' contains suggestions only – you or your teachers may have other ideas for researching conditions and context.

Area of Study 3: Developments in Instrumental Jazz 1910 to the present day	
Styles of jazz	**Suggested listening**
Early jazz	Jelly Roll Morton: *The Original Mr. Jelly Lord 1923–1941* Louis Armstrong: *The Best of the Hot 5 and Hot 7 Recordings*
Swing	Duke Ellington: *Never No Lament: The Blanton-Webster Band* Count Basie: *The Atomic Mr. Basie*
Bebop	Charlie Parker: *Ornithology – Classic Recordings, 1945–47* John Coltrane: *A Love Supreme*

Cool jazz	Miles Davis: *Kind of Blue*
Hard bop	Horace Silver: *Song for My Father*
Avant-garde and free jazz	Ornette Coleman: *The Shape of Jazz to Come* Evan Parker: *50th Birthday Concert*
Jazz-rock fusion	Weather Report: *I Sing The Body Electric*
Contemporary approaches to jazz	Maria Schneider: *The Thompson Fields* Courtney Pine: *Transition in Tradition*

Musical elements checklist

- Improvisation
- Swing
- Syncopation
- Polyrhythms
- Harmony and tonality
- Blues
- Blue notes and decoration of notes
- Timbre
- Organisation of pitch
- Devices – chorus, call and response, riff/ostinato
- Roles of solo and ensemble, rhythm section

Conditions and context	Topics for you to research and revise
The origins of jazz, New Orleans	■ Jelly Roll Morton, Louis Armstrong, Sidney Bechet and other New Orleans musicians.
Audiences in the US and Europe	■ The role of New York and Chicago ■ Duke Ellington's tours to Europe in the 1930s ■ Jazz in Britain after 1945.

Changes in popularity and commercial viability	▪ Use of electric guitars and keyboards in response to pop music.
Radio and recording	▪ Early recording technology ▪ The impact of the LP.
Working conditions	▪ Louis Armstrong's working life in 1920s New York and Chicago ▪ Jazz clubs in 1950s New York ▪ The decline of the big band after 1945.
Challenges for performers and composers today	▪ Case study of Maria Schneider: maintaining a big band, crowdfunding to fund recording projects ▪ Experiments in jazz composition.

Area of Study 4: Religious Music of the Baroque Period

Styles of religious music	Suggested listening
Catholic tradition in Italy	Claudio Monteverdi: Vespers Giacomo Carissimi: *Jephte* Antonio Vivaldi: Gloria in D major
Lutheran and Catholic Germany	Heinrich Schütz: St. Matthew Passion G. P. Telemann: Cantata – *Der am Ölberg zagende Jesus* J. S. Bach: St. Matthew Passion
Anglican developments	Henry Purcell: *Rejoice in the Lord Alway* G. F. Handel: *Messiah*
France	Marc-Antoine Charpentier: Te Deum in D J. P. Rameau: *Quam dilecta tabernacula*

Musical elements checklist

- Harmony and tonality
- Structures – recitative, aria, chorus
- Textures – chordal, fugal, imitative, solo and choral writing, instrumental
- Word setting, interpretation of text
- Resources, accompaniment (for example obbligato)
- Rhythm and metre, for example from dance patterns.

Conditions and context	Topics for you to research and revise
Worship and liturgy	- The role of music in Catholic worship - Music and drama in English and Italian oratorio - Changes in attitudes to instruments in the Lutheran church.
Dissemination of music, such as publishing	- Lully's control of music and its publication in France - Popularity of Handel's oratorios.
Working conditions	- Bach's cantata cycle for Leipzig - Westminster Abbey and the Chapel Royal.

Area of Study 5: Programme Music 1820–1910

Styles of programme music	Suggested listening
Concert overture	Mendelssohn: 'Hebrides' Overture Tchaikovsky: *Romeo and Juliet*
Symphonic poem	Liszt: *Les Preludes* Dukas: *The Sorcerer's Apprentice* Richard Strauss: *Don Quixote*

Programme symphony	Berlioz: *Symphonie fantastique* Liszt: 'Faust' Symphony Tchaikovsky: 'Manfred' Symphony
Solo works	Schumann: *Kinderszenen* Grieg: Lyric Pieces
Awareness of national identity	Mussorgsky: *A Night on a Bare Mountain* Sibelius: *En Saga*

Musical elements checklist

- Harmony and tonality, such as dissonance, chords, modulation for expressive effect
- Structure and expressive freedom
- Instrumental resources
- Dynamics, expression, articulation, complex textures, dramatic contrast and other effects.

Conditions and context	Topics for you to research and revise
The Romantic movement in the arts	- Shakespeare's influence on Berlioz - The Romantic approach to nature.
The influence of opera on concert music	- Effect of Wagner's operas on programme music.
Technological advances	- Developments in woodwind and brass - Piano technology and virtuoso pianists.
Audience, for example the middle class, industrialisation, railway travel	- Effects of industrial prosperity, such as the Philharmonic Hall in Liverpool, the Hallé Orchestra in Manchester - Dvořák and Mahler in New York.

Transmission of music, for example Europe and the United States, orchestras and public concerts	▪ Publishing houses, such as Breitkopf and Hartel ▪ Liszt's orchestra in Weimar.
Working conditions	▪ The role of the Paris Conservatoire in training French musicians ▪ The rise of the conductor.

Area of Study 6: Innovations in Music 1900 to the present day

20th and 21st century styles	Suggested listening
Late Romantic	Gustav Mahler: *Das Lied von der Erde* Sergei Rachmaninov: *Symphonic dances*
Impressionism	Claude Debussy: *La Mer* Scriabin: *Poeme de l'extase*
Expressionism, atonality and serialism	Alban Berg: *Wozzeck* Schoenberg: String Trio
Neo-classical developments	Stravinsky: *Symphony of Psalms* Francis Poulenc: Organ Concerto Dmitri Shostakovich: Symphony No.5
National styles	Béla Bartók: Music for strings, percussion and celesta Aaron Copland: *Appalachian Spring*
Post-1945 avant garde, experimental, electronic music, post-modern, e.g. Eastern/African influence	John Cage: *Sonatas and interludes for prepared piano* Luciano Berio: Sinfonia Harrison Birtwistle: *Endless Parade*

Minimalism	Steve Reich: *Different Trains* John Adams: *Shaker Loops*
Contemporary approaches to composition	Nicola LeFanu: String Quartet II Thomas Adès: *Asyla*

Musical elements checklist

- Irregular rhythm, metre, polyrhythm, polymetre, organisation of time
- Pitch, dissonance, harmony, tonality, modality, atonality
- Exploration of sonority, timbre, textures, instrumental and vocal techniques, resources, percussion, technology
- Dynamics, contrast, extreme range
- Structure, form, notation, improvisation, aleatoric.

Conditions and context	Topics for you to research and revise
Audience reaction to innovation	- First performance of Stravinsky's *The Rite of Spring* - Responses to avant-garde music in Europe and America.
Technology and mass media	- The role of the BBC in promoting new music - Early experiments in electronic sound.
Response of composers to political and social events, such as revolution, war, persecution and censorship	- Shostakovich's relationship with Stalin - Religious and pacifist expression in Britten's *War Requiem*.

The function and relevance of music, for example Gebrauchsmusik, crossover with popular styles, music for films, propaganda	▪ Korngold's film music for Hollywood ▪ Britten's music for children ▪ Prokofiev's music for Soviet film.
Working conditions	▪ The struggle for recognition for women composers ▪ Societies to promote new music (such as in Vienna) ▪ The developing musical culture of the United States.
Challenges and issues for performers and composers working today	▪ Case study of Thomas Adès ▪ Importance of film and commercial music in providing work for composers.

What the examiners are looking for

You are expected to show:

- Familiarity with the music:
  - analyse and comment in detail
  - choose relevant examples of music
  - use your knowledge of the music to make judgements.
- Familiarity with the context of the music:
  - analyse and comment on the background to the music
  - use your knowledge of the context to make judgements.
- Writing skills:
  - organise your ideas and develop your argument clearly and logically
  - answer the question
  - support your ideas with evidence.

All the essays are marked out of 25. The mark grid shows what examiners expect for each band of marks. As a guide, Grade A is about 20 marks, Grade E is 10 marks.

Marks	Knowledge and understanding of the background	Familiarity with relevant examples of music	Ability to make evaluative and critical judgements	Understanding of context	Ability to analyse and appraise
21-25	Thorough and detailed	Close familiarity with a wide range of examples	Good	Extensive	Clearly demonstrated
	Well-developed and sustained line of reasoning, coherent and logical in structure. The information is entirely relevant and supported by evidence.				
16-20	Specific	Close familiarity with a range of examples	Accurate	Good	Demonstrated
	Well-developed line of reasoning, clear and logical in structure. The information is relevant and mostly supported by evidence.				
11-15	Good	Some familiarity with some examples	Not entirely precise in detail	General	Not always demonstrated
	A line of reasoning, with some structure. The information is mostly relevant and supported by some evidence.				
6-10	Some, but relatively superficial	Some support from examples	Inconsistent in detail	Some	Partly demonstrated
	Some relevance, with limited structure. The information is supported by limited evidence.				
1-5	Some	Partly supported by familiarity with some music	Insecure, not always relevant	Very general	Weak
	Basic, unstructured. The information may be weakly supported by limited/unclear evidence.				

Answering the question

Top tips for Section C essays:

- If you leave Section C to the end of the exam, check how much time you have. You have two essays to write. Allow roughly equal time for each

- Read the questions carefully. Pay attention to the instructions telling you what to do – Explain, Describe, Evaluate, Analyse, Compare, Discuss

- Does the question tell you how many works or how many composers you need to refer to? Do you know enough music to answer the question?

- Choose two questions. They must be from different Areas of Study

- Write a quick plan, such as a checklist of important things in the order you want to discuss them

- Write a short introduction. This sets up the essay, showing the examiner in two or three short sentences that you have a clear idea of what you want to say

- Write in paragraphs and full sentences. Do not write in bullet points, even if you are short of time

- Begin and end with strong points, such as a clear opinion with good evidence. Hide weaker or shorter points in the middle. Don't let your essay tail off at the end

- Write in a clear, confident, formal tone – natural but suitable for a serious discussion. Use technical musical vocabulary when you can. You need to write quickly, so don't get tied up in complicated sentences with long words. Don't chat to the examiner (for example 'Sorry, we didn't study this topic!')

- Musical examples show that you know the music, but you only need a few. Use musical examples if they help to make your written answer clearer (for example to identify a motif or show the notes of a chord). Label answers clearly (Example A, Fig. 1, and so on) and refer to examples in your answer (such as 'see Example A', 'shown in Fig. 1').

Practice essay questions

Here are examples of the type of question in Section C. They are divided into four common types:

a. Musical styles

b. Musical elements

c. Conditions and context

d. Developing an argument and justifying opinions

Area of Study 3: Developments in Instrumental Jazz 1910 to the present day

a. Explain what is meant by the term 'cool jazz'. Illustrate your answer with examples from at least one jazz musician.

b. Compare the use of rhythm in early jazz and in later styles of jazz, explaining how the use of rhythm changed over time. Refer to at least three contrasting examples by different jazz musicians.

c. Explain the challenges facing a young musician attempting to make a living from jazz in the 1920s and 1930s.

d. Estimate the effects on jazz music of its gradual decline in popularity since 1940, with examples from recordings by two or more artists.

Area of Study 4: Religious Music of the Baroque Period

a. Identify and comment on the distinctive features of religious music in France in the Baroque period, with examples from at least one work.

b. Compare and assess the effectiveness of the choral writing of two composers in setting religious texts.

c. Outline the working conditions experienced by one composer of religious music of the period and explain their impact on at least one composition.

d. To what extent was Baroque religious music influenced by opera?

Area of Study 5: Programme Music 1820–1910

a. Explain the characteristics of a symphonic poem, referring to examples from at least two works.

b. Evaluate two works which make expressive or dramatic use of harmony to illustrate a programme.

c. Explain the similarities and differences between the working lives of composers from the first half and the second half of the period.

d. How important is it to be familiar with the programme when listening to programme music? Illustrate your answer with examples from three or more works of the period.

Area of Study 6: Innovations in Music 1900 to the present day

a. Discuss the importance of minimalism in contemporary music.

b. Evaluate two works which make striking or imaginative use of rhythm.

c. Assess the impact of persecution and censorship on the music of one (or more) composers of the period.

d. Identify one woman composer from the period since 1900 whose music deserves to be better known and explain why.

Writing answers to essay questions

Remind yourself of the advice contained in the sections above: What examiners are looking for (page 69) and Top Tips for Section C essays (page 71).

All essays need to demonstrate writing skills, whatever the question. Look for opportunities to show (i) familiarity with the music, and (ii) familiarity with the context of the music. How much of each will depend on the question you are answering.

The following table shows the ways J.S. Bach's cantata 'Wachet auf' can be discussed in response to different questions.

Type of question	Example – the chorale in Lutheran church music
a. **Musical styles**	**Example**: Describe the use of the chorale in one example of Lutheran church music. **Answer may refer to**: chorale melody used as cantus firmus in chorus of J.S. Bach's 'Wachet auf'; harmonised in 4 parts, SATB, homophonic to conclude the cantata.
b. **Musical elements**	**Example**: Comment on the harmony in chorale settings by one composer. **Answer may refer to**: for example Bach's 'Wachet auf' – strong diatonic harmony, E♭ major, clear perfect cadences, modulation to C minor, ii7–V7–I progression.
c. **Conditions and context**	**Example**: Explain the importance of the chorale in Lutheran church music. **Answer may refer to**: Protestant tradition, melody for congregation, well-known melodies/words (for example by Martin Luther), use in Bach's 'Wachet auf', reharmonisation.
d. **Developing an argument and justifying opinions**	**Example**: Comment on the effectiveness of the chorale settings by one composer. **Answer may refer to**: for example Bach's 'Wachet auf', skilful use of polyphony in the opening chorus, rich imitative texture, resourceful use of oboes and taille; strong harmonies in the final chorale, satisfying conclusion for the congregation.

Some of the information can be used to answer more than one question, but take care to read the question: sometimes exam candidates just want to write everything down, even if it is irrelevant. Make sure that you answer *the question in the exam paper*, not the question you wish it was.

Sample answers

Here are four extracts from sample essay answers. There is one for each of the Areas of Study 3–6. The extracts will give you an idea of the type of writing which is expected and how much detail you will need.

They are not perfect answers. The examiner's comments at the end suggest the strengths and weaknesses of each answer and gives an estimated mark for each.

a. Musical styles
AoS4

Identify and comment on the distinctive features of religious music in France in the Baroque period, with examples from at least one work. **[25 marks]**

Here is a section from the beginning of an answer:

Religious music in France in the Baroque period was mostly from the Catholic Church. Protestants were expelled from France during this period. Under Louis XIV France became more under royal power and everything was centralised around the court and the palace of Versailles. The King attended worship in the Chapelle Royale every day with music played and sung by his own musicians. He disliked listening to elaborate settings of the Mass, so a new type of music, the grand motet, was developed for the beginning of the service.

The 'motet a grand choeur' was usually a setting of texts from a psalm, arranged in separate movements for chorus (grand choeur), solo and duet/trio (petit choeur). The orchestra plays instrumental sections. The grand motet became a standard form in France, but often performed in concerts rather than in religious worship.

Rameau's 'Quam dilecta tabernacula' is an example of a grand motet. Only a few of his religious works have survived. It was written at a time when Rameau was a little-known organist, probably in Lyon between 1713 and 1722. He later moved to Paris and became famous for his operas and his theoretical writings. The style and structure of 'Quam dilecta' is similar to the motets of Lully, who dominated music in the 17th century. Lully's music, his influence under the patronage of Louis XIV and his control of the publication of music in France helped to create a distinctive French national style, which was copied by composers all over France.

'Quam dilecta' is a setting of verses from Psalm 84 (How lovely is your dwelling place). It divides into seven separate movements – Air, Choeur, Air, Trio, Récitatif et Choeur, Air, Choeur final. The work begins and ends in B minor, with the other movements in related keys: for example, the fugal chorus is in D major (relative major), the Trio returns to B minor, and the Recitative-Chorus is in G major. The words are repeated to make each movement a satisfying musical form. The motet lasts about 20 minutes, similar in length to other grand motets of the period.

The work is scored for chorus and soloists and an orchestra of strings, flutes and continuo. Flutes are often found in French music of the period. The flute is the first instrument heard in the opening air. The pleasant, pastoral sound matches the peaceful mood of the words.

The chorus is divided into four, SATB. The altos are marked in the score as 'haute-contre', a high tenor part in addition to the tenors. French pitch was lower than it is today, probably by as much as two semitones. The haute-contres often go up to A in the fugue (sounding as G), so this is not high for modern altos. Rameau divides the choir up further to create a richer sound. For example, in the double fugue he begins in four parts but later he divides the sopranos so that they sing in thirds.

At the end he divides the basses, using first basses as a harmony part and second basses to sing the bass. This creates a rich five-part texture for the homophonic passages at the end of the fugue. The fugue is a fast and exciting movement, using two themes and cleverly using stretto to bring entries of the themes closer together at the end. This is the only contrapuntal chorus. The other choruses are in a stately homophonic style, which is common in the music of Lully and Delalande.

The singing style is different from the styles of Germany or England. The Latin words are pronounced differently in the French style, for example in the Trio, where the word 'De-us' is sung almost as one syllable and with a different vowel sound on the 'u'. This can be heard clearly in the performance by William Christie and Les Arts Florissants. Another feature of the singing is the increased ornamentation of the melody. French musicians (vocal and instrumental) were expected to be familiar with a wide range of ornaments. The melody in the Trio looks very simple in the score, but the composer often adds appoggiaturas, mordents and trills to decorate the melody and make it much more expressive. Christie's trio of singers often add appoggiaturas to chords, creating interesting and expressive dissonance...

Examiner's comments on the answer so far:

- Well-written answer, showing clear knowledge of the French style. Some good comments on context (such as the importance of Royal influence), but also on Rameau as an example of composers outside Paris/Versailles

- Clearly knows 'Quam dilecta' well, with good detail on examples, some personal response to the music. References to Christie recording help to answer the question – relevant information on performance style. Some knowledge of other important composers

- Ideas are successfully organised into paragraphs. Moves easily from one group of ideas to the next.

Mark awarded for a complete answer: 22/25

b. Musical elements

AoS3

Compare the use of rhythm in early jazz and in later styles of jazz, explaining how the use of rhythm changed over time. Refer to at least three contrasting examples by different jazz musicians. **[25 marks]**

Here is a section from the beginning of an answer:

Early jazz and later jazz have different approaches to rhythm. The first examples of recorded jazz used syncopation. Audiences had never heard this before but it was very popular. In the 1920s swing was very popular. People used jazz for dancing in night clubs. It was played on the radio. After the second world war people stopped dancing to jazz because bebop was too fast.

In 'West End Blues' (recorded in 1927) Louis Armstrong begins with a trumpet solo, which was very difficult to play. He was famous as a soloist and lots of trumpeters copied his style of playing. He used swing rhythm in his playing. He played quavers as dotted notes – long, short, long, short etc. He used syncopation and his playing was not on the beat always. The rest of the band also played in this style. He used a rhythm section consisting of piano, bass, drums and guitar. The piano and guitar were comping, which means they were playing chords in crotchets. Dizzy Gillespie's 'Manteca' dates from 1951. This shows how the use of rhythm has changed. There is a very Latin rhythm to the piece, with lots of Cuban rhythms. This is because the composer Chano Pozo was Cuban. The rhythms are in the congas and add excitement to the piece. One of the main differences in rhythm from Louis Armstrong is the walking bass, which keeps the beat in crotchets by 'walking' up and down the scales and arpeggios. In Gillespie's music the drums play a swing beat on the hi-hat, using 'bombs' on the bass drum to interrupt the solo. This also happens in Miles Davis...

Examiner's comments on the answer so far:

- Some knowledge of the background and relevant points on rhythm in jazz. Understands some developments in jazz, makes some comparison of how jazz changes over time

- A few examples, mostly accurate, but limited, lacking detail, doesn't show that he/she knows this music well. The dates are wrong: West End Blues is 1928, Manteca is 1947.

Mark awarded for a complete answer: 7/25

This answer would be better if there were more detail and organisation of ideas, for example:

- Compare swing in Louis Armstrong and Miles Davis, for example anticipation of phrases, delay, double time, silence, with examples

- More on Latin rhythm in Manteca, such as description of full band and solo sections

- Discussion of the changing role of percussion, for example change from time-keeper to innovative style of Max Roach, Art Blakey and others – interplay with soloist, variety/pacing of accompaniment, examples of polyrhythm, development of the drum kit technique and so on

- A more recent example of jazz, showing new ideas about rhythm, for example Tito Puente Five-Beat Mambo.

c. Conditions and context
AoS6

Assess the impact of persecution and censorship on the music of one (or more) composers of the period. **[25 marks]**

Here is a section from the beginning of an answer:

I am going to look at the impact of persecution and censorship on the music of Dmitri Shostakovich. The examples are from Symphony No. 5, which he called 'a Soviet artist's reply to just criticism'.

Shostakovich was born in St Petersburg and educated at the Moscow Conservatoire as a pianist and composer. In 1917 the Russian Revolution took place. The Emperor was forced to abdicate and Russia began a period of rule by the Communist Party, led by Lenin. Under Communism, composers were controlled by the state and were expected to write music that could be understood by the workers. Shostakovich wrote many film scores and music that celebrated the revolution. For example his Symphony No. 2 has a large chorus singing the word 'October!'

In the early years of the Soviet Union Russian composers continued to be influenced by composers from Western Europe. The music of composers like Bartok and Berg was performed in Russia. One of Shostakovich's early successes was the opera Lady Macbeth of Mtsensk. It was a very dissonant opera. It followed the rules of the Communist party in that it was about ordinary Russian life, but the music was violent and harsh. The opera was very successful and had many performances in Russian opera houses. However Stalin (who replaced Lenin) attended a performance and he disliked the music. His views were printed in Pravda, the Communist party newspaper. The headline was 'Muddle Instead Of Music'. Shostakovich was very frightened about what was happening. Many people were being arrested, imprisoned and executed by Stalin. He expected to be arrested because of the controversy about his opera.

The Fifth Symphony was his way of becoming accepted as a composer once again. He needed to demonstrate that he had listened to the criticism of the Communist Party and was prepared to write the sort of music that the party required. Therefore the first movement is in a clear sonata form and the rest of the symphony follows what is expected of a symphony: four movements, including a scherzo and a slow movement and a fast and triumphant finale. The melodies are easy to follow and the harmonies are not as difficult as his earlier works. The opening theme has a dramatic leaping melody in a dotted rhythm, the cellos and basses are answered by the first violins. The steady tempo sets a serious, expressive tone. There is no sign of the wild, adventurous style that angered Stalin...

Examiner's comments on the answer so far:

- Clear and informed writing. Good knowledge of the background, some specific detail on working conditions for Soviet composers
- Relevant and accurate reference to the music. Successfully links the music with its historical background, making sensible judgements and answering the question
- Well written. Good organisation of material into paragraphs, ideas flow in a logical sequence
- Sometimes lacks detail, such as dates, reference to Moscow and St. Petersburg, more on the work of the Composers Union. Knows the music well, can comment on expressive and technical features, but not detailed enough for the highest band of marks.

Mark awarded for a complete answer: 18/25

d. Developing an argument and justifying opinions

AoS5

How important is it to be familiar with the programme when listening to programme music? Illustrate your answer with examples from three or more works of the period. **[25 marks]**

Here is a section from the middle to the end of the answer. The works being discussed are Berlioz: *Symphonie fantastique*; Fanny Mendelssohn-Hensel: *Das Jahr*; Richard Strauss: *Don Quixote*:

Compared to the Symphonie fantastique, Fanny Hensel's Das Jahr (The Year) has a less obvious programme. Written in 1841 this is a sequence of 12 piano pieces, one for each month of the year from January to December, and a postlude. The programme works as a journey through the year, but each month has an accompanying quotation. Although she wrote The Year after journeying through Italy, there are references to German poets and quotations of chorale melodies from the German Lutheran church.

'September' is taken from a poem by Goethe – Flow, flow, dear river. Never will I be happy'. The flowing semiquavers (beginning in the right hand) are maintained throughout the piece without a break. The key of B minor suggests the unhappy story of the poem. The song-like melody in the middle of the texture expresses the sadness of the woman standing by the river. The harmony shows the depth of feeling. It modulates to G# minor, then has the G# as a bass pedal for four bars before making an enharmonic modulation to Db major. The middle section has an extended passage in Bb minor with a tonic pedal. The melody is based on a chromatic phrase – A, Bb, Cb, B – exchanged between the left hand (decorated with the flowing semiquavers) and the right hand in octaves. The final section returns to B minor with the return of the opening music, as if nothing has changed and the music dies away (marked 'calando') at the end.

The next piece, 'October', is a complete contrast – a lively hunting piece. The text refers to the forest and the joyful sound. The broken chords music suggests the sound of hunting horns. The music changes between common time and 6/8 sections. There is a strongly diatonic harmony, very different from the expressive chromatic harmony of 'September'.

The programme of the work – the months of the year – is very clear and easy to understand. There is also a clear contrast between each of the individual pieces. Even if the text at the beginning of the piece is not known, the mood or character of the piece is expressed clearly. German audiences would also be able to follow the chorale melodies. In 'December' the melody of 'Vom Himmel hoch' is quoted at the end and people would know this as a Christmas hymn.

A different approach to the programme is found in Richard Strauss's symphonic poem Don Quixote (1897). The music is based on the novel by Miguel Cervantes. Like Berlioz, Strauss wrote a detailed summary of the programme. The music is structured as a theme and ten variations, with a long introduction and finale. Each variation is a different part of the story. A solo cello represents the character of Don Quixote, with the viola representing Sancho Panza, his servant.

Strauss illustrates the story in as much detail as possible. Don Quixote has three themes to show different aspects of his character. 1 The little opening fanfare melody in the woodwind represents his knightly behaviour. 2 The grazioso melody in the violins represents his courtesy; 3. The descending chromatic chords represent his slippery delusions. In addition Strauss has a huge orchestra to illustrate the scenes vividly. The sheep in variation 2 are shown in the dissonant flutter-tonguing of the woodwind and brass. The music is quiet at first, with the violas divided into desks and the woodwind playing a shepherd's tune. The fanfare theme in the bass shows Don Quixote charging at the sheep, the dissonance and fluttertonguing becomes louder and more urgent as the sheep scatter.

The three examples show different ways of using a programme. Strauss's programme is much more detailed than Berlioz or Hensel's. It is impossible to follow most of the music of Don Quixote unless you are familiar with the programme. The music is strongly associated with the character and the situations in the story. In some ways this is also true of Symphonie fantastique: the idee fixe represents a character in the story, and the titles of each of the movements give a sense of the story. While The Year has some programme elements there is not such as strong sense of the story and the individual pieces can stand alone much more easily.

Examiner's comments on this section of the answer:

- Mostly thorough and detailed knowledge of the background, specific examples of context, very good understanding of the issues in answering the question

- Close familiarity with the music of Hensel's *Das Jahr*, detailed and specific examples of techniques in the music. Less detail on *Don Quixote*, but shows some familiarity with the music

- Able to organise ideas logically and draw conclusions from each work. Good attempt to discuss and compare in the final paragraph.

Mark awarded for a complete answer: 22/25

Chronology

Here is a list of key dates and events for the two compulsory Areas of Study: Areas of Study 1 and 2. This would form a good starting point for your revision.

Area of Study 1: Instrumental Music of Haydn, Mozart and Beethoven	
Haydn 1732–1809 **Mozart 1756–91** **Beethoven 1770–1827**	
1761	Haydn takes the position of court Vice-Kapellmeister with Prince Paul Anton Esterházy. He is employed by the Esterházy family for the rest of his life.
1762	On the death of his father, Prince Nicolaus I Esterházy succeeds. He builds a new summer palace at Esterháza.
1766	Haydn becomes Kapellmeister, in charge of all the music at the court.
1773	Mozart takes up a position as court musician at Salzburg for Prince-Archbishop Colloredo. He resigns in 1777 but returns in 1779.
1779	Haydn signs a new Esterházy contract which allows him to accept commissions from elsewhere and to have his music published.
1781	Haydn's 6 string quartets, Op.33, 'written in a new and special way'. Published by Artaria in Vienna in 1782. Mozart quarrels with the Archbishop and is dismissed. He settles in Vienna, with the aim of working freelance.
1782	Mozart begins a series of successful subscription concerts (until 1785), with himself as soloist in his own piano concertos.
1785	Artaria publishes Mozart's 6 string quartets dedicated to Haydn (composed 1782–85).

1789   The French revolution overthrows the monarchy in France.

1790   Death of Prince Nicolaus I Esterházy.

1791   Haydn's first visit to London, at the invitation of J.P. Salomon.
Haydn meets Beethoven in Bonn on the journey and on the way
back. Haydn writes 12 symphonies for subscription concerts
in London (1791–2 and 1794–5). Mozart writes his final works,
including a Clarinet Concerto, K.621 for Anton Stadler.

1792   Beethoven arrives in Vienna.

1795   Publication of Beethoven's set of piano trios, Op.1, dedicated
to Prince Lichnowsky. The profits are enough to pay his living
expenses for a year.

1797   After a series of defeats against Napoleon's army in Italy,
Austria makes peace with France. In 1799 Napoleon becomes
First Consul, effectively dictator of France.

1804   First performance of Beethoven's Symphony No. 3 in E♭ 'Eroica'.

1809   Vienna is briefly captured by the French. Under the Treaty of
Schönbrunn, Austria gives up some of its lands in exchange for
peace.

1814   Napoleon is defeated by the Allied powers. He abdicates as
Emperor of France and is exiled to Elba. He returns to power in
1815, but is finally defeated at the Battle of Waterloo (1815).

1824   Beethoven's last public concerts, including the first performance
(in Vienna) of the Ninth Symphony (commissioned by the Royal
Philharmonic Society in London).

Area of Study 2: Popular Song: Blues, Jazz, Swing and Big Band

1910   First experimental public radio broadcast (Enrico Caruso and other singers, from the Metropolitan Opera House, New York).

1923   Bessie Smith makes her first recording, 'Downhearted Blues', for Columbia Records. It sells 780,000 copies in the first 6 months.

1927   Broadway premiere of *Show Boat* (music by Jerome Kern, words by Oscar Hammerstein II) – considered the first modern American musical (compared to musical comedies/follies).

1929   Wall Street Crash. Collapse of the Stock market and beginning of the Great Depression. 13 million unemployed in the US.

1931   Bing Crosby's solo radio debut – a weekly programme of 15 minutes.

1934   *The Gay Divorcee* – the first Fred Astaire movie with Ginger Rogers.

1944   NBC begins network television broadcasts, linking New York, Washington and Philadelphia.

1948   Columbia record company introduces 12-inch Long Play (LP) microgroove disc, playing at 33 1/3 rpm. RCA Victor issues a rival 7-inch 45prm disc. Both formats are widely adopted as standard – the 7-inch for singles, the 12-inch for albums.

1964   The Beatles' first US television appearance on The Ed Sullivan Show is watched by 73 million viewers.

1982   The first releases on compact disc (CD).

Glossary

Acciaccatura. A very short ornamental note played just before a principal melodic note.

Anacrusis. The note or notes that form an upbeat (or upbeats) to the first downbeat of the phrase.

Anticipation. A non-chord note that is approached by step and then stays the same as the following harmony note.

Antiphony. A texture where two instrumental groups or two choirs alternate in dialogue.

Appoggiatura. An ornamental note that falls on the beat as a dissonance and then resolves onto the main note.

Arpeggio. A chord in which the notes are played one after the other rather than at the same time.

Articulation. The way in which a series of notes is played with regard to their separation or connection. For example, staccato (separated) or legato (connected).

Atonal. Western music that is not in a key or mode. Often dissonant.

Augmentation. The lengthening of rhythmic values of a previously heard melody, or the widening of an interval.

Augmented chord. A triad that has an augmented 5th as the top note instead of a perfect 5th.

Augmented 6th. A chord that contains the interval of an augmented 6th above the bass note.

Auxiliary note. A non-harmony note that is a step above (upper auxiliary) or below (lower auxiliary) the harmony note and returns to it.

Binary form. Two-part structure (AB), usually with both sections repeated.

Broken chord. A chord in which the notes are played one after the other rather than at the same time.

Call and response. A pair of phrases, performed by different musicians, in which the second phrase is heard as a reply to the first. This term normally refers to jazz, pop and world music.

Chord extension. Chords that contain additional intervals to the 3rd and 5th degree of a triad, creating a 7th, 9th, 11th or 13th chord.

Chord inversion. A chord that has, for example, the 3rd or 5th as the bass note instead of the root of the triad.

Chromatic. The use of non-diatonic notes (notes that are not in the current key).

Circle of 5ths. A series of chords whose roots are each a 5th lower (or a 4th higher) than the previous one. For example, Em–Am–Dm–G–C.

Compound metre. Time signature in which the beat divides into three – for example, $\frac{6}{8}$, $\frac{9}{8}$, $\frac{12}{8}$.

Conjunct. A melody which moves by step.

Consonant. Intervals or chords that are stable and sound pleasant (for example, unisons, 3rds, 6ths) as opposed to its opposite, dissonant.

Con sordino. With the mute. Usually seen on music for string instruments.

Continuo. Short for 'basso continuo', the continuo instruments form the accompaniment in Baroque music. It may include instruments such as the harpsichord (capable of playing full harmony) and a cello and bassoon reinforcing the bass line.

Contrapuntal. See counterpoint.

Contrary motion. Movement of two or more parts in opposite directions to each other.

Countermelody. An independent melody that complements a more prominent theme.

Counterpoint. A texture in which two or more melodic lines, each one significant in itself, are played together at the same time. When describing this texture, you would use the adjective contrapuntal.

Diatonic. Using notes that belong in the current key.

Diminished 7th. A four note chord made up of a diminished triad plus a diminished 7th above the root.

Diminution. A compositional technique in which the durations of a motif or phrase are proportionally reduced in a restatement of it.

Disjunct. A melody that moves in leaps rather than by step.

Dominant 7th. A four-note chord built on the dominant (5th) note of the scale. It includes the dominant triad plus a minor 7th above the root.

Dominant pedal. A pedal note on the fifth degree of the scale of the prevailing key.

Dotted rhythm. A rhythm that contains pairs of notes in the pattern 'long-short'. The first note is dotted and the second is a third of the dotted note's value (e.g. dotted crotchet – quaver)

Double-stopping. A string technique of playing more than one string at a time.

Fugue. A contrapuntal composition in which a short melody or phrase (the subject) is introduced by one part and successively taken up by others and developed by interweaving the parts.

Fugato. In the style of a fugue, but not in strict or complete fugal form.

Glissando. A slide between two notes.

Grace note. A quick ornamental note that comes before a main note.

Ground bass. Repeating bass, usually four or eight bars in length, with changing music in the other parts. Popular in Baroque music.

Harmonic. Sometimes known as a flageolet note, a technique of lightly touching the string (e.g. on a violin) to produce a high flute-like sound.

Harmonic sequence. The restatement of a harmonic passage at a higher or lower pitch.

Harmonic rhythm. The rate at which harmony changes in a piece.

Homophonic. A chordal texture in which one part has the melody and the other parts accompany. In contrast to a polyphonic texture, in which each part has independent melodic interest.

Imitative. A contrapuntal device in which a distinct melodic idea in one part is immediately copied by another part, often at a different pitch, while the first part continues with other music. The imitation is not always strict, but the basic rhythm and melodic outline should be heard.

Imperfect cadence. The end of a phrase harmonised with two chords, the second of which is a dominant chord.

Interrupted cadence. At the end of a phrase, a dominant chord followed by almost any chord other than the tonic chord. The second of these chords interrupts the expected resolution of the dominant chord to the tonic.

Interval. The distance between two notes. For example, the interval between the notes F and A is a 3rd (A is the third note of the F major scale).

Key signature. A group of flats or sharps placed immediately after the clef at the beginning of a stave or immediately after a double bar. These flat and sharp signs indicate which notes are to played flat or sharp whenever they appear on the same stave (unless they are contradicted by accidentals).

Legato. A smooth articulation of music without any breaks between successive notes.

Leger line. Additional lines used above or beneath the stave to represent notes that fall outside of its range.

Marcato. Accented notes, played with emphasis.

Melody dominated homophony. A texture consisting of a melody with chordal accompaniment.

Melodic sequence. The restatement of a melodic passage at a higher or lower pitch.

Mode. Seven-note scales that can be created using only the white notes of the piano keyboard. The dorian mode can be played on D (i.e. D–E–F–G–A–B–C–D), the mixolydian on G, the Aeolian on A and the Ionian on C. These interval patterns can then be transposed to any other note. For example, dorian beginning on G (or G dorian) would be G–A–B♭–C–D–E–F–G.

Modulation. The process of changing key.

Monophonic. A musical texture that uses a single melodic line.

Mordent. A melodic ornament of two types: a) the lower mordent, which consists of the written note, the note a step below it and the written note again, and b) the upper mordent, which consists of the written note, the note a step above it and the written note again.

Octave. An interval formed from two notes that are 12 semitones apart. Both notes have the same name.

Ornaments. Small musical additions that decorate a melody, e.g. trill, mordent, acciaccatura, appoggiatura.

Ostinato. A repeating melodic, rhythmic or harmonic motif, heard continuously throughout part or the whole of a piece.

Passing note. A non-essential note filling the gap between two notes a 3rd apart.

Pedal note. A sustained or continuously repeated pitch, often in the bass, that is heard against changing harmonies. A pedal on the fifth degree of the scale (known as the dominant pedal) tends to generate excitement, while a pedal on the key note (known as the tonic pedal) tends to create a feeling of repose. A pedal that is not in the bass but at a higher pitch is known as an inverted pedal.

Perfect cadence. A dominant chord followed by a tonic chord at the end of a phrase.

Phrasing. In performance, the execution of longer groups of notes that follow the natural patterns of the music. 'Articulation' may be used to refer to phrasing over a shorter group of notes. Phrases may be indicated by the composer but the skill and judgement of the performer is also important in creating a successful performance.

Pitch. The height or depth of a note. Pitch can be measured in absolute terms by counting the number of vibrations per second of the source of the sound, e.g. A (above middle C) = 440Hz.

Pizzicato. A direction to pluck notes on a string instrument.

Plagal cadence. A subdominant chord followed by a tonic chord at the end of a phrase.

Polyphonic. A texture consisting of two or more equally important melodic lines heard together. In contrast to a homophonic texture, in which one part has the melody and the other parts accompany. The term polyphonic has a similar meaning to contrapuntal, but is more often used for vocal rather than instrumental music.

Portamento. A slide between two notes.

Relative minor/major. Keys that have the same key signature but a different tonic. The tonic of a relative minor is three semitones below the tonic of its relative major (e.g. C major and A minor).

Riff. A short catchy melodic or rhythmic idea that is repeated throughout a jazz or pop song.

Ritornello. A Baroque device where the repeated tutti section is used as a refrain; most often in the first or last movement of a concerto, or in arias or choral works.

Ritornello form. Standard form of first and last movements of the Baroque concerto, alternating tutti ritornelli with solo or ripieno (small group) sections.

Rondo form. A main theme (sometimes called the 'refrain') alternates with one or more contrasting themes, generally called 'episodes' (ABACADA etc).

Rubato. The alteration of rhythm, particularly in a melodic line, by lengthening or shortening notes but keeping an overall consistent tempo.

Scale. A sequence of notes that move by step either upwards or downwards. Different types of scales have different patterns of intervals.

Sequence. Immediate repetition of a melodic or harmonic idea at a different pitch, or a succession of different pitches.

Sforzando. Strongly accented.

Simple time. A metre in which the main beat is sub-divided into two equal portions (e.g. a crotchet beat divided into two quavers). Opposite of compound time.

Sonata form. Typical first movement form of the Classical and Romantic periods. In three sections – exposition, development, recapitulation – often based on two groups of melodic material in two contrasting keys (first subject, second subject).

Staccato. Detached. Refers to notes that are held for less time than their values indicate, so they are shortened and separated from each other.

Subdominant. The fourth degree of a diatonic scale.

Suspension. A dissonance that occurs when the harmony shifts from one chord to another, but one or more notes of the first chord (the 'preparation') are either temporarily held over or are played again against the second chord (against which they are non-chord notes) called the 'suspension.' The suspended note is then 'resolved' onto a note in the following chord.

Syncopation. Placing the accents in parts of the bar that are not normally emphasised, such as on weak beats or between beats, rather than in the expected place on strong beats.

Tempo. The speed of the music.

Ternary form. A musical structure of three sections. The outer ones are similar and the central one contrasting (ABA).

Texture. The relationship between the various simultaneous lines in a passage of music, dependant on such features as the number and function of the parts and the spacing between them.

Tonic pedal. A pedal note on the first degree of the scale of the prevailing key.

Tremolo. A musical effect that refers to a very quick and continuous repetition of a single note (on bowed or plucked string instruments) or of two alternating notes (on keyboard instruments).

Trill. An ornament consisting of a rapid alternation of two adjacent pitches.

Triplet. A group of three equal notes played in the time normally taken by two of the same type.

Turn. A four-note ornament comprising the note a step above the written note, the written note, the note a step below the written note and the written note again.